Power Communication
Secrets of the Alpha Male Book 2
by Drawk Kwast

I0454741

Drawk Kwast | The Alpha Male Advantage
Reality is a crutch for those lacking enthusiasm and imagination.

Published by Drawk Kwast Holdings, LLC
3565 Las Vegas Blvd. South, Suite 241
Las Vegas, NV 89109
www.drawkkwast.com

Printed in the United States of America on acid-free paper.
ISBN: 1479372706
ISBN-13: 978-1479372706
Library of Congress Control: 2012918186
©2012 Drawk Kwast Holdings, LLC
All rights reserved.

Contents

Part Seven: Humor

Introduction

You and I are known by many names: rebel, heathen, and seducer, to name a few. Why do they call us these names? At some point, we found the box that society wanted us to live in very uncomfortable, so we abandoned it. At this point, most of us don't even remember what the inside of that box looked like, but we remember how painful it was, and we know we're never going back. They told us that life outside of the box would be difficult, yet we flourished. They continue to call us irresponsible, reckless, and unprofessional as we enjoy a life of money, women, and power far beyond their reach. We may live by a forbidden code, but ours is a group for which membership is open to anyone with the balls to join and brains to thrive. As I write this, I assume that you are already one of us. If you are not, this book may be your only chance to join us.

What you hold in front of you right now contains the secrets we use to communicate our ideas in such a powerful way that it changes the reality of how much money we earn, who we date, and what we have influence over. You are about to embark on a journey beginning with the simplest core concepts and leading to an understanding of the very nature of reality itself.

First Things First

If you worked your way through my first book, *Domination Basics: Secrets of the Alpha Male Book 1*, you already know that this second book is about to make everything else on your bookshelf look like Dr. Seuss. This second book is built on the important and very necessary foundation of *Domination Basics*. Without understanding the basics, you're not equipped to handle what's inside this book. I want you to get the maximum value out of what I've written and receive the rewards for following these instructions. To do that, you must first read:

Domination Basics: Secrets of the Alpha Male Book 1
by Drawk Kwast

ISBN-10: 1453801898
ISBN-13: 978-1453801895
LCCN: 2010915248

Available at **www.drawkkwast.com**
and wherever books are sold.

How to Read This Book

This book is organized into eight parts. Your first instinct will be to read it cover to cover, but realize that no one can digest and integrate this material into their lives that fast. This book was written to be read one part at a time, with one week between each part to put what you have read into practice. Remember to take notes and use a highlighter as you work through each part, building a clear plan of how to apply and use each week's lessons. This book wasn't written to be read. It was written to be done. Wise men recognize that the wisdom comes from doing, not simply from reading. Do every task, and practice, practice, practice. Different people will get slightly different things out of this book, based on the experiences it leads them through. This is your adventure for the next eight weeks and, if you do it correctly, for the rest of your life. Live it well.

Power Communication Part 1
Linguistics

Week 1

When we communicate, it all starts with our thoughts. When we choose to speak, we have a mechanism in our brain that references the library of words in our head and decides what words will best convey the thought. If the thought is weak, the mechanism by default chooses weak words. If the thought is strong, the mechanism by default chooses strong words. Communicating with power requires the use of strong words, and strong words require strong thoughts. We build strong thoughts by using strong word choices, both for conversation with others and for conversations with ourselves (better known as thinking). This may seem like circular logic, but in fact this is the cornerstone for linear thinking. Your thoughts and words function in a symbiotic relationship. Think of it as linguistic algebra. Whatever happens on one side of the equation must be balanced on the other side.

Consider the following sentence:

I wrote a book. Some people said it was alright, so basically I figured I'd try writing a second book.

Compare that to this:

> *People frequently comment on the clarity and insight of my first book. I felt led by my readers to write a second book.*

Now if I were asking you to buy a presale copy of this book, which example of word choice would better serve my purpose? The answer is obvious.

Part one of this book covers the art and science of word choice. As you become a master of this, you will shape your communication in a way that displays power and confidence, increasing your ability to persuade others. You will also be able to decode the word choice of other people and have a deeper glimpse into their thoughts. After some practice, you will make an additional discovery: the link between word choice and thought is a two-way street. A person who masters word choice will also master his unconscious thought. A person who has mastered his own unconscious thought can then learn to influence the unconscious thoughts of others, most of the time without others even being aware of it.

Weak Words for Lazy Minds

There is a list of words that people use as a way to avoid committing to their own ideas. Weak language is a reflection of a person's lack of confidence in his own ideas. It's OK to be wrong on occasion. It is not OK to be generally unsure of yourself. There are times when these words are a necessary and normal part of speech, such as when you are talking about other people who are always uncertain of themselves. In general, however, you can omit these words from your speech. Some examples of these words are *usually*, *probably*, *most likely*, *often*, *basically*, and *typically*. Consider the difference between the following statement and the effect it would have on a new client:

> *Basically, I do good work. My clients are usually happy with the results I produce.*

Compare that to this:

> *I do good work. My clients are happy with the results I produce.*

Considering the first example, how comfortable would you feel if this statement were coming from your neurosurgeon right before your operation? In these examples, you can see the effect weak language has on your perception of the doctor's abilities. His self-doubt is blatantly obvious.

Negative Statements

Another type of weak language is negative statements. It takes a bit of explanation on how the brain works to understand this concept. The unconscious brain cannot understand negatives. Negatives can be processed only by your conscious brain. Here's a simple example. If I tell you to stop thinking about a pink elephant, what do you start thinking about? A pink elephant. How does this happen? When I say, "Don't think of a pink elephant," your conscious passes the pink elephant part to your unconscious. Your unconscious passes an image of a pink elephant back to your conscious, and your conscious says, "OK, don't think about that." If we are at the circus and I don't want you to think about elephants, it's much more effective to just say, "Hey, look at the clown." Here are some further examples of negative statements and how to correct them:

I don't want to go to McDonald's for dinner.

I can't believe how you are behaving.

Change to:

I would rather go to Sizzler for dinner.

I had more respect for you five minutes ago.

Try

The word *try* is implied failure. Has someone ever said something like the following to you? "I tried my best and won first place." No, he just tells you that he won. Yoda was right when he said, "Do or do not; there is no try." To illustrate this further, let's do the following experiment:

Try to pick both of your feet up off of the floor.

How did you do? Did you try? It's impossible. You either did or did not pick your feet up off of the floor. Do not use the word *try* in any reference to yourself. If you are uncertain of the outcome, simply talk about your next step.

Do not let other people use the word *try* with you when working toward a common goal. If others use the word *try* with you, they are unconsciously telling you that they intend to fail. Don't let them get away with that. Have them rephrase the statement using different words, and your chance of success goes up.

One of the more interesting things you can do with *try* is to use it to take power out of other people's statements. For example:

They say: I am going to become an astronaut after college.

You say: You can try.

In this case, using the word *try* is like peeing on their campfire. It ruins their campfire, and the smell is awful. Remember that *try* kills statements by infecting them with doubt.

Why

The use of *why* in your life is now completely prohibited (unless you use it as part of a joke). Some of the people I work with have a running joke about the word *why*. If one of us spills a drink, that person will exclaim in the whiniest voice possible, "Whhhhyyyyyyyyy?" This is our way of making fun of the people who still use this word. I can hear you asking, "But why can't I use *why*?"

The problem with the word *why* is that it has no personal power. A man loses his job and spends hours crying to his friend, using an overdose of the word *why*. A woman finds out her husband has been cheating on her and uses the word *why* an obscene number of times between the massive crying sessions. *Why* usually has no other point than whining. Replace the word *why* with *how* and you regain power and find resolution. *How* covers the series of events leading up to the problem. At the very least, you can learn from that. The man lost his job because he always came in 15 minutes late. That is *how* it happened. The husband cheated on the wife because she put on 45 pounds since their wedding, and that is *how* that happened. Mystery solved, conversation over, next question please. Anything that moves you to logically answer your *how* question with a *because* gives you the power to learn from it and move on. Don't let people use *why* with you anymore. Tell them that you no longer understand it, and ask them to use the word *how*.

Soon

From the movie *Spaceballs* (1987):

Question: When will then be now?

Answer: Soon!

The word *soon* doesn't actually tell you anything. In most cases, when someone uses the word *soon* as a response, he may have just as well said, "Shut up!" Push people for a real answer.

*A man asks the office's secretary if she can have his contracts completed and ready for submission by the end of the day. She replies by saying that she will **try** to have it done **soon**. When people put* try *and* soon *in the same sentence, your response must be the same as if they just told you that you should set your wallet on fire and hope for the best. The man instructs the secretary to make the same statement without use of* try *and* soon. *The secretary responds with a schedule of events. She explains that there are four contracts in front of his and that if they take an average amount of time to complete, his will get done. The man has accomplished two things because tractable expectations have been set. First, he can make an* *educated guess on the likelihood of this getting done. Second, he has increased the likelihood of this getting done because he has limited the stalling points. If any reason other than the one she gave prevents the work from being done, she will have some explaining to do.*

Should and Could

The word *should* implies the presence of a negative or questionable thought. When used in the past tense, the implication is that you have not figured out what went wrong and thus you have not yet learned anything, so you have some research to do. When the word *should* is used before executing a plan, people perceive that you are unsure. If people tell you that you "should" do something, ask them the details of **how** they arrived at that conclusion. Here are some examples:

> *That should have worked. vs. That did not work; let's do this.*

> *That should work. vs. That has an 87% chance of working.*

> *You should dump your girlfriend. vs. Dump your girlfriend because I want to date her.*

When you use the word *should* in self-talk, you are either thinking too much or not enough. If you say to yourself, "I should have enough money in the bank to pay my bills," you have some research to do. Figure it out. If you say to yourself, "Should I be kissing this girl now?" you are too much in your own head. The answer is YES, so just do it, right now.

Could is very similar. Let's reuse one of the above examples:

That could work. vs. That will work.

Don't be lazy. Do your homework. Know what you are getting into, take action, and figure it out. If you tell me I have two options for saving my own life and either could work, expect me to ask some questions. Demonstrate by word choice that you know what you are talking about and what to do. Be a leader.

Hope

One more word to stop using is *hope*, because it's the battle cry for people who have decided to do nothing. The problem with the word *hope* is that it becomes an action, the action of sitting on your ass hoping rather than taking another action that does something productive to move you toward your goal. Think of it like this: if two people are faced with a problem, and one person tells you they "hope" things work out and the other tells you his action steps for resolving the problem, which person do you think has a better chance of conquering that problem?

I hesitate to go from the profound to the profane here, but my grandfather put it best. Grandpa once asked me, "If you hope for something with one hand and shit in the other, which hand will fill first?" This definitely demonstrates the weakness of the word *hope*.

Can and May

Now that we have discussed some of the words you don't want to use, let's look at some words that are acceptable, as long as you understand how to use them. Two examples are *can* and *may*. *Can* is a question of possibility while *may* is a question of permission. Confusing the two only shows a lack of understanding of the English language. Here is an example:

> *"Can I kiss you?" WRONG! I am sure you are physically able to kiss her!*

> *"May I kiss you?" Partially correct, at least from a viewpoint of proper grammar.*

Do not use these words unnecessarily because doing so shows weakness. In my example above, the phrase "May I kiss you?" is wrong because asking only kills the mood by showing uncertainty. Most failed kisses are from a lack of certainty. If the question "Should I be kissing her right now?" enters your head, the answer is yes. The time is now. Do it before you think and become uncertain.

One of the biggest mistakes you can make with the word *can* is to use it to check someone's beliefs about you. Do not ask your friends, "Do you think I can get that job?" It's their belief, which is completely irrelevant. In addition, this is just an attempt to seek validation, which shows self-doubt. The question itself is also flawed. The better question would be "Do you have any advice that will help me during my job interview?" Seek advice, not validation.

Next, let's consider the following example:

Can you pass me the potatoes?

Please pass me the potatoes.

When you want someone to pass you the potatoes at the dinner table, ask him *to* pass the potatoes, not *if* he is able to pass the potatoes. The other thing you will notice is that the first way is a question while the second is a statement. We will discuss later in this book why statements are always better than questions.

What

The important thing to understand about the word *what* is the two primary modes in which it's used. The first mode is clarification. If I make a statement and people cannot understand me, either because they did not hear me clearly or because I used a word they don't understand, they will respond with "What?" The second mode is confusion. If I give instructions using words that people hear and understand the meaning of, but still somehow they cannot comprehend my message, they will also respond with "What?" Never confuse the two situations. Doing so gives away your power, as this example shows:

A man walks up to an absolutely gorgeous group of women and says, "Would you ladies like to buy me a drink?" One of them responds with "What?" This woman heard exactly what the man said. She is just so blown away by the question that her autopilot response is "What?" If she can get him to repeat himself, she has time to think of a zinger of a response.

But

But is a very interesting word. I'm not going to tell you to stop using it, **but** I am going to show you how to properly use it. The word *but* is a destroyer. The general structure of any sentence with the word *but* in it is as follows:

Statement #1, BUT Statement #2.

The word *but* has a basic function, and that is to destroy whatever thought proceeded it. Consider the difference between the following two sentences:

Gary, you're a cool guy, but I don't want you dating my sister.

Gary, I don't want you dating my sister, but you are a cool guy.

Whatever the last thought is will hold the most weight. Both options convey the same information, but the impact on Gary will be different. If you intend to be harsher with him to be sure he gets your point, use the first option. If your intent is to let him down easy, go with the second option. If your sister is turning him down, it may sound more like the following sentence:

> *Gary, I'd love to go out with you on Friday, but I have to wash my hair.*

Emphasis – Last Thing Said

The examples above with *but* show the concept of the last thing said holding the most emphasis. This is a common rule in rhetoric. When a sentence is put together, the item or thought at the end holds the most importance. Think of it like the conclusion of a story. It's all about the ending. The following example shows how the order of the words affects their meaning:

Max taught Spanish to the students.

Max taught the students Spanish.

The first version is about Max and his students. Spanish becomes a connector merely explaining the relationship. The second version is about Max teaching Spanish. The students are merely the necessary people involved for Max to do so. Now that you understand the structure, let me give you a more relevant example.

The girl Jake just took out on a date comes home and tells her roommate "I just went horseback riding with Jake." Groovy for Jake; he was more important than the horse. If she says "Jake" and then "horseback riding," you know she had more fun with the horse than she did with Jake (HINT: Ways to spot a gold digger).

41

When you speak, be sure to get the order of your thoughts correct. Always arrange them to benefit yourself in terms of your audience, as this example will show:

Just sign here. I will take care of everything.

I will take care of everything. Just sign here.

The first option will get you more signatures. The second option will make more people wonder if you are just saying that to get the deal.

Sometimes you will use this as a tool of humor and to be playful. Consider the following list of sentences:

You have beautiful eyes.

I hate you.

Pass the guacamole.

You have perfect hands.

Now consider how these same statements have been completely changed by the addition of a different ending.

You have beautiful eyes. Can I hold them?

I hate you. Let's cuddle.

Passing me the guacamole would be awesome!

You have perfect hands for giving me a backrub.

They now have a totally different meaning. In the example "You have beautiful eyes," we may have added the ending to rescue ourselves from a compliment gone wrong. If you are on a first date with a girl and want to kiss her, you may *try* doing it by leaning in and telling her she has beautiful eyes. When she realizes that you want to kiss and she is not into the idea, she will pull away, at which point you add the "Can I hold them?" part to the end. She now thinks that you are just being silly.

In the second example, you may be kidding around with your girlfriend, who just bought you a gift. At first she thinks that you are displeased, and thus it makes the reward even better when you tell her a half-second later that you like it and want to cuddle.

In the third and fourth examples, we have come up with a playful way to make a request of someone. With the backrub example, if we simply ask for a backrub and get turned down, we look weak. However, if we do it as we did in the fourth example and get turned down, it's no longer rejection. It becomes a joke. The less people see you getting rejected, the more they will feel inclined to go along with your requests. When you master this game, it will appear that everyone goes along with whatever you are suggesting. The more people believe that, the more inclined they will be to simply go along with whatever you are suggesting. This is incredibly powerful.

Modal Operator Statements

Like a word or phrase that adds an important twist to the plot of a story, Modal Operator Statements change everything surrounding them. They give ideas context. Some examples are *if*, *yet*, and *up until now*. Here are two examples:

> *If I were to tell you I love you, how would you respond?*

Note that I did not actually tell her I love her.

> *A certain situation has never happened here, yet.*

What does the *yet* imply? It opens a world of possibilities. This simple tool allows you to remove the power from statements other people make when you don't agree with them.

When someone else makes a statement, you have the option of adding *if* before the statement or *yet* at the end of the statement to effectively take the power out of the original statement. Optionally, you can use *if that were to happen* at the end of the statement to create a redirected statement that has less power. Consider the following example:

Girlfriend: I've never given you a reason to doubt me.

You: Up until now.

Consider your opening statement if you were to ask a Fortune 500-type boss for a raise. I have listed four such statements in ascending order of effectiveness.

> *Please give me a raise.*

> *Give me a raise.*

> **Up until now**, *I have not received a raise.*

> *If you gave me a raise, my wife would not mind me putting in additional work hours.*

The first option sounds like you do not deserve it. The second uses no tactics. The third makes a positive assumption. The fourth proposes an option that is a win/win for all. Also take note that *please* can be added to the base statement *give me a raise,* but once you deploy tactics, it would be very hard to work a *please* in. This is because *please* works only with questions, and we are building statements. We will go into great detail on questions vs. statement later, in part five of this book.

Presuppositions

Presuppositions are statements in which some unstated element must be assumed (presupposed) to be true in order for the statement to make sense (to be true or false). Going back to the example above on how to get a raise, the best option is to presuppose a win/win by replacing *if* with *when*.

> ***When*** *you give me a raise, I'll be able to work more hours and have my wife smiling about it.*

The first thing this does is assume that you will get the raise. Then it constructs a win/win. From the company's position, not only will you be working more hours, but your wife will also not be nagging you to get home from the office. In fact, the way you have presented it suggests that even if you want to come home, your wife will encourage you to stay. This is a powerfully confident and persuasive statement.

When building presuppositions, use suggestions rather than commands. Commands will be stopped by your audience's conscious minds. Suggestions slip straight into the unconscious and do their work quietly. This tactic is among the most powerful verbal kung fu you can use.

Now some of you will be saying that the statement is made weaker by the fact that this person is mentioning his wife, as if he cannot do whatever he wants. You are completely correct. Getting married is a loss of power. By definition, once you are married, it's team play, and you now make decisions together. Team decisions are a presupposition of marriage. Do you want to get an idea of how powerful the presuppositions of marriage are? Just ask a new bride what her husband just agreed to without his knowledge. I could write a whole book on *A Man's Guide to the Presuppositions of Marriage*. The only problem is that if men knew what they were in for, they would stop getting married.

Some more examples of presuppositions are:

"Of course, I am just one man, and that is just my opinion. Others with less experience are free to think otherwise." – Mark Twain

Presupposition: Those who think otherwise have less experience.

I get mad only when you get stupid.

Presupposition: You are stupid.

You will know it happened when you hear a sudden loud noise.

Presupposition: It will happen.

Either get smart or be quiet.

Presupposition: You are saying something dumb.

You will feel a little tickle in your pants when you think of me.

Presupposition: You will think of me.

You turn the cutest shade of red when you are embarrassed.

Presupposition: You are embarrassed right now.

Stop looking at me that way. You're too young for me.

Presupposition: You are attracted to me.

I give this pen only to clients who are ready to sign.

Presupposition: If you are holding this pen, you are ready to sign.

The power of the presupposition is the same power that exists in the "don't think of a pink elephant" example. It's very sneaky and just slips in there. Once it's in, it can run amok in people's unconscious mind without them even knowing it.

Final Thoughts

Be careful and be easygoing with the information you just read. My goal here is to make you conscious of your word choice, not turn you into a stuttering fool who overthinks every word. Be fully conscious and fully relaxed at the same time. That's how this game is won.

In conclusion, remember that every time you choose a word, you are shaping your identity. You may be talking about yourself, someone else, or something else, but your word choice **ALWAYS** reflects the identity you have chosen for yourself. Change your words and change your identity. The result is a powerful shift in the way people respond to you.

Power Communication Part 2
Paralinguistics

Week 2

When we communicate, there are the words we choose, and there is the way in which we use them. Word choice is called linguistics, which is discussed in part one of this book. The style we communicate the words with is paralinguistics. Think of linguistics as everything that is in the dictionary plus a handful of grammatical rules. Think of paralinguistics as an opera with a symphony orchestra behind it, minus the actual words. Paralanguage modifies the meaning of language and conveys the speaker's emotions.

In written words, we actually see paralanguage with our eyes. For example, if I print the word *important*, it tends to trigger a dictionary definition in most people. However, if I use that same word but type it in all big, bold, red capital letters, it will modify the definition for most people to include a "take caution" message of some sort, like that of a warning sign.

In spoken words, we hear the paralanguage with our ears. The paralanguage of speech includes everything but the words themselves (ignoring body language, which we will talk about in the next part of this book). This is also called the nonsemantic aspect of speech. For example, a voice can be male or female.

A person can talk fast or slow. A person who is trying to talk while crying has a certain sound. A confident person has another distinctive sound behind his words. In normal communication, how things are said is about five times as important as what is said. This is why paralinguistics is so important to understand.

How would you describe your own paralanguage? Does your voice suggest calmness, patience, annoyance, interest, sensitivity, or weakness? How is it perceived by others? The interesting thing about paralanguage is that most people have an easy time reading it from others, but they are almost clueless to the paralanguage they communicate. Do you remember the first time you listened to a recording of your own voice? I'm sure you responded, like everyone else, by saying that it sounded nothing like you. News flash: When you listen to a high-quality recording of yourself, that is exactly what you sound like to everyone else. The really amusing part is that what you think you sound like sounds nothing like you. The reason is that your brain's microphone is mounted to your body's speaker. When someone else hears your voice, their ears pick up vibrations only from the air. When you hear yourself, your ears pick up vibrations from the air, but they also pick up the vibrations from being directly physically attached to the same head. The acoustics are totally different. When you hear a recording of yourself, you experience the acoustics in the way everyone else does.

Record Yourself

The first step in gaining control over your paralanguage is to record yourself and listen to it. The number one tool you will use to fix your language, paralanguage, and body language is a video camera. Once you understand the rules of language, paralanguage, and body language, you can become self-correcting with the help of a video camera. Working on your presentation in this way is not easy because you will see the flaws that you did not know you had. If you are reading this, you are probably interested in fixing yourself. That's great news! Now the hard part: get over your childish ego, bring your problems into the light, and deal with them. I didn't say it was easy; I said it was progress.

Record yourself. Record every situation you possibly can. Athletes do this all the time to discover things they can improve on. Record yourself doing physical activity. If your answer to that is that you do not do physical activity, start five minutes ago and get video of it. Get video of yourself at work giving presentations. Record your phone calls (to keep things legal, tell the person that you are recording for "training purposes"). Get footage of yourself with your kids or nephew, or go visit a friend who has kids and record yourself showing them how to use a yo-yo. If you are single, have your date or girlfriend record you (as part of the date; you're just playing with the camera). If you are by yourself, use a tripod to record yourself rocking out (singing along to your favorite songs) while folding your laundry. Be creative and just do it. Now that we have that covered, let's learn what you are watching for.

Speed

In general, the less people believe someone is interested in listening to them, the faster they will talk. If you have ten minutes of stuff to say but believe you can hold your audience's attention for only five minutes, you will want to talk twice as fast as usual. The problem with this idea is that everyone else's unconscious knows this rule. What happens is that the faster you talk, the more people believe that you yourself do not believe what you are saying is valuable. As a result, they tune you out more than they would have if you had just talked more slowly.

If you naturally tend to talk fast, as is the case with people who think visually, learn to slow it down. Know that by slowing down, you will be more easily understood. If you have a high IQ, be aware of the fact that most people do not think as fast as you and thus cannot listen as fast with comprehension. It's not so much that they are slow as much as it is that *you* are *fast*.

Filler Words

If a person believes he is going to lose his audience's attention, he does not leave moments of silence in his speech. He thinks that if he leaves a gap of silence, he will lose the attention of whoever he is talking to. On the other hand, people who believe they have captivated their audience's attention will purposely leave breaks with silence to build suspense. Breaks with silence and pauses convey confidence. Generation of constant sound shows a lack of confidence. Remember that a pause for thought is OK. You do not need to say "uh" when you are simply taking a breath as you build your next thought. Pausing to take a breath is a part of normal conversation. Filler words are ANY words or sounds that do not need to be there. Know that if 20% of what is coming out of your mouth is filler words, your message just got much more than 20% weaker. Not only are the filler words wasted space in what you're saying, but they also make the words next to them weaker. The more filler words you use, the less people will value what you say. Popular examples of filler words are *uh*, *um*, *er*, and *ah*. These are not words! Stop using them. Other good examples are *um, OK* and *know what I mean?* added onto the end of statements. Every time someone ends a statement with *know what I mean?*, I answer "no" and then ask him to explain himself better.

My all-time most hated filler word is *like*. I loathe the use of this word. If ever you wanted a word that completely destroys any brilliant articulation, this is the word. It's best to stop using it completely and replace its occasional necessary use with *similar to*. I have a twenty-year-old friend who loves this word. Every time he uses it with me, I interrupt and tell him that I do not want to know what something is "like" but rather how <u>exactly</u> it is. Slow down your speech and you will notice that filler words disappear.

Pronunciation

Knowing the proper pronunciation of words is essential for conversations with intelligent people. Intelligent people will quickly dismiss others as less intelligent when they hear words pronounced incorrectly. It is very true that different countries speak English with slightly different stylistic modifications from the British original, but that is not what I am talking about. I am talking about people who have no idea what the pronunciation key in a dictionary is. I blame political correctness for letting this one happen. We've been taught that if people sound like morons, it would be rude to tell them. Not telling people only perpetuates the problem. Most who mispronounce words do not even know they are doing it.

If you are a professional new to an industry, be sure you know the proper pronunciation of the industry's jargon. Screwing this up is like holding a sign in all your meetings that says, "I don't know what I'm talking about."

The solution can be found at most online dictionaries that have sound clips of the proper pronunciation for any given word.

Emphasis

Part of proper word pronunciation depends on what syllAble you put your emPHAsis on. The pronunciation key in a dictionary can tell you what part of a word gets emphasized. The next thing to understand is how emphasizing a particular word in a sentence changes the meaning of that sentence. Read the following sentence out loud and put emphasis on the bold word as you do.

How are you feeling today?

How **are** you feeling today?

How are **you** feeling today?

How are you **feeling** today?

How are you feeling **today**?

Can you hear the meaning change slightly? If you ask the above question with emphasis on the **you**, people will be more inclined to think that you really care about them, or possibly that you are a secretary who asks this question of 400 people a day. If you put the emphasis on the **today** part, people's unconscious will tend to ask the question, "As opposed to what, yesterday?"

You can also pay attention to what part of a conversation holds the most weight for someone by where the person puts the most emphasis. I love this game with employees when they are explaining how something went sideways. You can pick up on vocal cues the same way a lie detector works. When they get uncomfortable, uncomfortable = emphasis, and that is the part of the conversation you want to focus on. The emphasis will be on what they are lying about.

Pitch

When pitch is adjusted throughout a sentence, it works like emphasis, as in the above example. Let's look at the following interaction:

Bob: Where do you want to go for lunch?

Jim: I would like to go to Burger King.

Because the above is written in plain printed text, you read it as a simple question and statement. Consider for a moment how things change if Jim were to say the "Burger King" part with a slightly higher pitch than the rest of the sentence. Jim's statement becomes more of a question to Bob. It's like saying, "Burger King, if that is OK with you." Raising your pitch at the end of a sentence makes you sound unsure of your statement and turns it into a question.

When it comes to your default pitch level, practice lowering your pitch without putting too much effort into it. Alpha males tend to have deeper voices.

Variation

In the movie *Ferris Bueller's Day Off* (1986), there is a scene where Ferris' teacher is taking roll. Ferris is not in class, and the teacher keeps saying, in the most boring monotone voice possible, "Bueller... Bueller... Bueller..." Don't be that guy. No one listens to "that guy" for very long. A good conversationalist, a good storyteller, and a good teacher all have one thing in common. They all know how to hold the audience's attention with variations of their paralanguage. Keep things lively by varying speed, tone, and emotion in your voice as it matches the ideas you are talking about, without overdoing it. There is a happy medium between Ferris Bueller's monotone teacher and a televangelist selling Jesus.

Projection

Most of the people who come to me for live training have problems with vocal projection. Vocal projection is not something you are going to learn from reading about it, but I can give you a few good tips to point you in the right direction.

Your voice starts with your breathing. Most people breathe very shallowly. Watch yourself as you breathe. If your stomach is moving, you are doing it right. If your chest is moving and not your stomach, you are breathing shallowly. You must breathe slowly and deeply, totally filling your lungs with each breath. Practice it now. Breathe in until you cannot take in any more air, and let your stomach fully expand out as you do. Now that you have an idea as to how much air you can take in, release it and inhale again, but don't exaggerate it. Just comfortably fill your lungs, and let your stomach expand out as you do it. Now you have what you need to project your voice.

The next thing to know is that the sound starts from your diaphragm at the bottom of your lungs, not the back of your throat. With every word you make, push it from deep inside the bottom of your lungs. Screaming will be felt in your head and neck while proper vocal projection is felt more in your chest and lungs.

Humans have evolved different responses to the two methods of vocalization. When someone screams, humans go on alert and become uncomfortable. When someone speaks loudly in a commanding voice, humans pay attention and become ready to follow instructions. If you want to test this, go to a public place, such as a mall. Stand 20 feet from someone else who knows how to properly project his voice without screaming. Have a conversation, and at some point, without changing actual volume, replace the projection method with screaming and watch the massive difference in the people around you. It will go from paying attention to becoming unsettled. When you have mastered vocal projection, you will be able to have conversations in public from literally 40 feet away without unsettling those around you.

Posture counts, so stand up straight, hold your head high, and keep shoulders back. The more you crumple up what is used to produce your voice, the weaker it gets. When I talk with people on the phone, I can hear in their voice if they are standing or sitting. If they are standing, I can hear if they are walking, slouching, bending over, or maintaining good posture. If they are sitting, I can hear how good their posture is. The better their posture is and the further their knees are from their shoulders, the less constricted their airflow is and the more powerful they will sound.

Learn to Sing

To truly become a master of paralanguage, you must learn how to sing. Remember what I just said about people getting uncomfortable when listening to a recording of their own voice? Well, it's worse when it's a recording of yourself singing. Again, I'm asking you to let go of your ego in the pursuit of excellence for yourself.

What most people don't understand about singing is that the words are only a conduit, a way to express the emotions the singer is feeling in that moment. Most people who try singing for the first time in public are very nervous. That is the emotion they feel, and that is the emotion that gets pushed out. The result is horrible singing. The secret to learning how to sing is to simply get over your ego and practice letting your emotions loose through the words. When interviewing singing teachers, tell them your goal is to learn to sing with passion and emotion. You will know you've got it when it feels good.

That sums up paralinguistics. Start by reviewing recordings of yourself and use the information you just read to self-correct. Master your paralanguage by learning to sing in public. Always sound like you have just as much right to talk and be heard as anyone else, because you do.

Power Communication Part 3
The Art of Physical Space

Week 3

When you walk into a room, you speak before you say your first word. Whether it be confidence or self-doubt you hold, it's instantly on display as shown by how you take up physical space. You can read a hundred books on body language, yet somehow the true self always shines though. If you succeed at stopping one nervous mannerism, your body betrays you as it finds a new way to display your discomfort.

You are about to learn the art of physical space. Your journey begins inside of yourself, where we will change the way you look at the physical world around you. Changing how you feel about your surroundings, and then letting your true self shine though, is the only path to rock-solid poise. You will then understand that how you hold your body and what you do with the physical objects around you are all determined by what's going on inside your head.

Just how important are these spatial games we play in society? Mehrabian's Rule tells us that 55% of our communication is how we take up physical space (body language), 38% is how we say things (paralinguistic), and only 7% is what we say (linguistic). So you can look at it like this: if you've mastered parts one and two of this book but don't master this third part, you're not going to get very far. It's time to add a third dimension to your communication arsenal.

Environment

Powerful body language is about being comfortable in any environment you choose to enter or happen to find yourself in. It says that I've been here before, I know what to do, and everything will be alright. For a moment, I want you to consider the concept of "environment" from a scientific point of view rather than a social one:

> *We know from physics that it is impossible for two objects to occupy the same space at the same time. We also know from physics that by definition, the space around any object is its environment. If two objects are next to each other, each is still in its own environment, physically speaking. It is impossible for one object to be in another object's environment without it being in its own environment at the same time. Two objects in the same environment share that environment.*

For some reason we lose sight of this concept when we stop talking about objects and start talking about people. Wherever you are *is* your environment. Wherever other people are is their environment. Their environment and your environment are the same environment when you are in proximity with them.

You can directly, physically affect things only in your environment. You cannot directly, physically affect things that are not in your environment. So any place where you can directly, physically affect things is your own personal environment.

If I enter your house at your invitation for dinner and sit at your table, most people would say that I am in your environment; but if I tip my glass over and spill the wine on your table, what does that say? I have directly, physically affected something (my glass), so I must be in my environment to do such a task. Look further at the statement "tip my glass over and spill the wine on your table," and you will realize something else somewhat amusing. This statement is made in the most common way that most people would say it. There exist three items: a table, wine, and a glass. Next let's look at the implied ownership as stated, remembering that all of the items actually belong to you. The phrase "your table" indicates that it is yours. Next is "the wine," implying that it is not yours but open to anyone, which is interesting because you bought it. Last, and most amusing, is "my glass," which indicates that it is mine, despite the fact that you bought it and it is in your house. True, you gave it to me to use when you set it inside my "personal space," which in itself is a very interesting concept because my personal space is currently at your table.

The point of this discussion is to show you that the concept of "environment" as we use it socially is a huge, confusing gray area, open to social interpretation.

> *There are two women sitting at a table in a bar. One of them gets up to go to the bathroom. Just as she does, a man walks into the bar. The man sits in the empty seat. The woman at the table explains that he can't sit there because it's her friend's seat. The man explains that the seat belongs to the bar and not her friend, and furthermore, he is quite capable of sitting there, proven by the fact that he is. The woman tells him to take a hike and that her friend is going to be upset if she comes back and sees him in her seat. The man explains to her that as soon as his sister gets out of the bathroom, she will be happy to see him. This is the first time the woman has met her friend's brother.*

Is the woman in the bathroom her friend or his sister? Who's the actual owner of the seat? Every story has at least two sides. Reality is a gray area. The reality of any environment is open to interpretation, followed by conquest. The strongest reality always wins.

So why is this concept so important to understand? Because the idea of being in someone else's environment is nothing more than a decision to yield power to the other people sharing the environment with you. The idea is that you move freely through your environment, which is anywhere you find yourself, and which can also be someone else's environment. It's never a matter of invading the enemy's environment. It's more like marking your environment, which is wherever you find yourself, and then deciding how you want to share that environment with others. Truly understanding the implications of this at an unconscious level will completely change your reality and your entire life. For those who understand, no further explanation is necessary. For those who do not, no other explanation is possible.

Respect

One of the more interesting parts of my job isn't giving powerful psychological tools to guys, but rather teaching them how to use these tools properly. Sometimes I feel like I am giving atomic weapons to children. For those who truly understand what I have just given you, we need to talk about respect for a moment. I have just given you a Swiss Army knife. You will spend the next few years figuring out everything you can do with it. I just need to be sure you don't do anything dumb like cut off your own finger or take apart my television while I'm not looking.

What you have just read on the concept of environment is not telling you to disrespect anyone (including, and most importantly, yourself). Offer everyone a base level of respect at first but no more, and no less. As you share an environment, you will adjust as you have logical reason to.

Everyone wants respect. Respect is a funny thing though. Respect is always given. You cannot make people respect you; they have to give you respect. People who think they can force others to respect them are creating fear, not respect. Your presence must result in respect for you, not fear of you. Fear is completely unnecessary if you have respect. If too many people fear you, they will eventually group together to disassemble the source of their fear, you. If people respect you, they will band together to make you stronger.

Being Neutral

The body language of a true Alpha Male is very simple. It can be summed up in the following sentence: **An Alpha makes every move deliberately, with conscious purpose, and without rush or apology.**

When an Alpha walks into the room, the first sign of his confidence is his speed and style of approach. It's slower and more deliberate. He never appears to be nervous or jumpy, and he isn't putting too much effort into anything. He keeps his composure at all times. He is centered and stable. When Alphas walk, they lead from the hips, with more of their weight on their heels. Most people look like they are about to fall over when they walk, with their head and chest ahead of their body catching the weight on their toes. Alphas keep their spines in alignment and their heads back. They are floating rather than having their back and neck muscles always fighting to keep them from falling over. The result is fewer back and neck problems, and the result of that is a happier person. You can achieve perfect Alpha posture by practicing the Alexander Technique (pull this one up on Google).

Whether you are looking at it from the Eastern perspective of having your chakras aligned, or from the more scientific Western perspective known as chiropractic, you need to get your spine in alignment and keep it there for health reasons that most people don't even know about. All the nerves that go out into your body get there through your spine. The nerves exit your spine through the spaces between your vertebrae. When your spine is out of alignment, the spaces can close too much on one side, and the result is pinched nerves. If a set of nerves going to your heart, for instance, gets too restricted, your brain has trouble communicating with your heart, resulting in heart problems. I never went to a chiropractor myself until I was about 27 because I never thought I needed it. I stood up straight and worked out at least six days a week. A friend of mine who I found out was a chiropractor encouraged me to come in for a free visit and some x-rays. I was amazed when he took one look at my x-rays and told me that I had lung-related issues and slept too much. I admitted to getting bronchitis about twice a year but told him I liked the sleeping thing. After chiropractic treatment, I don't get bronchitis anymore. So go find a chiropractor and get some x-rays. You may find out that your stomach problems are because your T6 vertebra is out of alignment.

Desensitization

One of the quickest ways to help get your body language to neutral is through desensitization. Dogs wag their tails when they are happy. It's a trait in canine body language, and they don't even know they do it. When you bring a new puppy home for the first time, what does he do? He wanders around sniffing and scouting the place out. He is nervous from being unsure of his environment, and because of this won't be wagging his tail. As soon as he gets comfortable, he starts wagging his tail again.

When you walk into a situation you are not normally in, you do not wag your tail, so to speak. There are all kinds of things you do that shout out, "I'm not comfortable." Rather than giving you a long list, I can much more effectively teach you how to become comfortable. Would it be easier to train that puppy to wag his tail when he's nervous, or would it be easier to simply make him comfortable so he does it naturally and automatically? It is the exact same with you, and we can make you comfortable through desensitization.

Here is an example of some desensitization work I did with one of my clients:

One of my clients had problems giving presentations at work. Here is how we fixed it.

First we took him to a lesbian bar and taught him how to make friends. Next we had him give a 20-minute presentation on "The Danger of Potatoes" that we prepared for him (think Monty Python in a boardroom). On the third day, we had him give his last business presentation to us (the last one he actually gave at his company) while one person randomly shouted obscenities at him and another played with Nerf toys in our rented meeting room. It took some work, but he finally made it through all three while being able to hold his composure. He got a promotion five weeks later.

The basic idea of desensitization is to put yourself in the situations you have not been in enough for the purpose of becoming used to them. It helps to practice situations that are exaggerated so that the real thing seems to be even easier.

Motivation for Unnecessary Movement

Every problem you will ever have with body language can be fixed by asking three questions: "What are you doing?" "Why are you doing it?" and "Is this beneficial for you?" Most people do not know all of their nervous twitches and mannerisms. As I said in the last part of this book, get a video camera and record a ton of footage of yourself. Get video of yourself at work giving presentations. Get footage of you with your kids or nephew, or go over to visit a friend who has kids and record yourself showing them how to use a yo-yo. Have your date or girlfriend record you, as part of the date, just playing with the camera. If you are by yourself, use a tripod and record yourself rocking out to your stereo while doing laundry.

Next, ask yourself why you are displaying certain mannerisms. Are you being playful or boring? Do you look nervous or stressed? Do you look in control? Look for all the little things. If you have a friend who plays poker well, ask him to help find your tics. If you do not know why you are doing something, such as blinking a lot when you can't find your car keys, you simply stop doing it! No unnecessary movements! Have a reason for every movement you make. If you are a nail biter, stop. Even if people do not see you biting your nails, they can see the results of your doing it, and that advertises weakness. Type "stop nail biting" into Google and take care of that. Put "I need a drink" and "I need a cigarette" into this same category. The reason people develop nervous habits is simply to give them something to do to help take their mind off of their discomfort when they are nervous. If you need something to do when you're nervous, completely focus on your breathing. Some will know what I mean by that last statement, but most will need to study Zen meditation to figure it out.

Diet and Exercise

The bodies that we have today are a product of evolution. Most of that evolutionary time was spent hunting for meat, gathering fruit and vegetables, and running for our lives as bigger animals hunted us.

The only diet that makes any sense is called the Paleolithic diet (look this up on Google) because it is the only diet that gives your body what it needs based on how your body evolved. As a very basic explanation, our ancestors didn't have Twinkies 40,000 years ago, and because of that, your body today hasn't evolved to digest Twinkies in a healthy way. Our ancestors ate meat, fruits, and raw vegetables, which our modern bodies have had thousands of years to adapt to.

Your body has evolved to eat meat. If 40,000 years ago, a group of people decided to become strict vegetarians, they would have died out. There was an evolutionary advantage to eating meat. The first was that not eating meat meant less available food. The more food options you had, the greater your chances of having enough to eat and therefore, to survive. The second was that the more protein you ate, the better shape your muscles were in for hunting food and protecting yourself and your family from other animals hunting you. If you happen to be one of these people who think humans should not eat meat, you are probably only one step away from telling us that we should not walk because it's hard on our feet and cite calluses as your scientific reason for this conclusion. If you think meat is murder, I will agree with you while I put more A1 on my T-bone steak. Try taking that steak away or telling me I shouldn't eat it, and I'll eat you. Alphas eat meat.

Your body has evolved to eat fruit and raw vegetables. This ability gives you more food options and gives your body nutrition that it cannot get from meat alone, some of which is vital to things like your immune system. Don't ruin your vegetables by cooking all the nutrition out of them. Vegetables have far less nutrition after you cook them. If you hate the idea of eating your vegetables, buy a juicer, which extracts nutrition from fruit and vegetables for fast and easy consumption. To give you an example, you would be crazy to eat two pounds of raw carrots in one sitting. With the help of a juicer, you can get the nutrition in two pounds of carrots by drinking one glass of carrot juice. You'd be amazed at how well your body repairs itself when you're drinking a half bushel of raw organic vegetables a day (but go easy on fruit, which is high in calories). Alphas eat fruit and raw vegetables.

As for the things you need to stop eating, at the top of that list is soy and high fructose corn syrup, followed by anything else considered "food" but made in a lab. I put soy at the top of the list because it loads your body with estrogens, which is never a good idea for men. If you happen to be one of these idiots who think soy is safe because Asian cultures have been eating it for thousands of years, you are very wrong. They eat traditionally fermented soy products in small amounts as a condiment (only 1.5 % of the calories in a Chinese diet). Modern soy foods are very different from those consumed traditionally in Asia. Most are made with soy protein isolate, which is a protein-rich powder extracted by an industrial process from the waste product of soy oil manufacturing. This process also uses a completely different soybean. The soybean consumed today has been bioengineered and is not the same as the one used by traditional Asian cultures. For the full story, Google "dangers of soy."

As for high fructose corn syrup, it has replaced safer natural sugar and has been loaded unnecessarily into an unbelievable amount of popular foods. Some of the reasons to avoid high fructose corn syrup are significant risk of obesity, increased risk of developing type-2 diabetes, hypertension/elevated bad cholesterol levels, liver damage, and mercury exposure. As a good rule of thumb, start reading the labels on the food you eat, and if you don't know what an ingredient is, look it up on Google. It is amazing to me how clueless people are about what they put in their bodies. It's true that you are what you eat, and most people walking around are petri dishes of bioengineered sugar, unnatural hormones, and chemical food preservatives. Not good. You only get one body, and in my opinion it is well worth the time to educate yourself on how to properly feed it. Buy a book on the Paleolithic diet.

Your body has evolved to do strenuous physical activities. When you consider what your ancestors had to do on any given day 40,000 years ago, it amazes me that people think five hours of exercise a week is asking too much. Alphas work out at least five days a week for at least one hour per day (warm-up, looking at cute girls, and showering not included in that time). Alphas go to the gym.

So what does any of this have to do with body language? A very high percentage of what gives an Alpha his body language comes from the above things. Eating right and working out regularly provide many positive results. You will feel better, look healthier, and reduce stress. Your self-confidence will grow, women will become more attracted to you, and you will naturally be more dominant. All of these things play a huge part in how you carry yourself.

Chances are good that if you are not exercising in some way for at least one hour a day, five days a week, you are fat and/or out of shape. Not sure if you're fat? Most fat people don't think they are fat because of the totally screwed-up, politically correct society we live in today. The only thing that gets me more confused than fat people walking into a McDonald's is why I am not supposed to call them fat. I know it makes them feel bad. If a doctor knew I had cancer but figured that he didn't want to tell me because I might get upset, I would call that doctor a fool. To know for sure where you're at, get a body fat test done at your local gym. If they do the pinch test with the calipers, make sure they use at least five sample spots. The most accurate test out there is the one where they dunk you in a tank of water. That test is on a truck that drives from gym to gym and stays at each place for a few days. Again, just ask about the dunk tank body fat test at your local gym. Look at the results and get on a program to deal with it. On the other end of the spectrum, if you are one of these skinny-as-a-rail types, the body fat test will show you that you don't have enough fat to be healthy and that you need to start eating normally again.

Now let's look at a basic way to determine your fitness level outside of body fat. Have the gym check your VO_2 max. This is a test of your cardiovascular system's ability to transport and use oxygen. Remember, as you read the results from your body fat and VO_2 max tests, your goal is not average, which is fat and out of shape for Americans. Your goal is somewhere between healthy and ideal.

It's What's on the Inside That Counts

The outside of a person is a direct reflection of what's on the inside. Do I feel bad for stupid people living with the results of their own stupidity? No. How about lazy people living with the results of their own laziness? No on that one also. Then why would I feel bad for a fat person who is living with the results from a combination of laziness and stupidity? People are fat on the outside from a combination of laziness and stupidity on the inside. Just as anorexic people's bodies are a direct reflection of their inner problems, so is being fat. The same can be said for 99.9% of "ugly" people (excusing only those with extreme birth defects and survivors of drastically disfiguring physical trauma).

The saying "It's what's on the inside that counts" is the motto for people who have given up on themselves. The way a person looks is a direct reflection of knowledge, inner strength, and discipline, which all has a compounding effect over a lifetime. No one living on raw broccoli and organic chicken breasts (without sauce), drinking only filtered water, and exercising an hour a day will stay fat or ugly. Have a common health condition? The answer can be found in modern medicine. Can't afford it? Put effort into earning the money to afford it.

Many years ago, a small number of people could persuade me to feel guilty for my harsh black-and-white views on this. It never happens anymore. What changed? I met two amazing women. The first was a roommate of a good friend of mine. I didn't believe her when she told me that she used to weigh over 300 pounds. She went on to tell me that she underwent a combination of gastric bypass, liposuction, and a series of plastic surgeries to remove excess skin. How did she pay for it? She wasn't rich. She worked at a Wal-Mart. She worked and saved for years to accomplish this.

The second girl I met at my gym. I caught myself lusting after her from across the room so I walked over to strike up a conversation. After a few minutes and a few smiles, she told me that she worked out so hard because she used to be 240 pounds. We have since become friends, and I've verified her story, which I didn't originally believe.

The most interesting thing about both of these women (besides their incredible willpower) is how confident and friendly they both are. Because they used to be so overweight, they had to develop great personalities to survive in this world. They obviously couldn't get by on looks they didn't have. The result now is that they look great and have awesome personalities.

Clothing and Grooming

As we discussed in "Diet and Exercise," when you look good, you feel good, and looking/feeling good dramatically changes your body language automatically. Part of looking good is a matter of clothing and grooming. We can learn everything we need to know in this area by asking three questions: "Why do you look a certain way?" "What does that say about you?" and "Is it a benefit?" If you are like me, you have facial hair because real men have facial hair. If you shave your legs, you are either a woman, bicyclist, swimmer, or gay. Ultimately, this is the structure to use to discover and build your identity:

If you _____ , it's because you

_____ .

The above sentence causes you to discover motive for everything you do. Put thought into everything. It all comes down to reasons, and remember that your saying, "I don't care," is never an acceptable reason.

So start with trimming your nose and ear hair. Buy a tongue scraper. Keep your nails cut and clean. Straighten and whiten your teeth. You need to practice relaxing your jaw and lips so people don't see stress in your face, and that means they are going to see some of your teeth, so you'd better get them in "show shape."

Get a tan. Your goal here is to look like you get about one hour of sun per day and no more. If you actually do this by being outdoors, be sure to use a sunscreen that blocks harmful UV light. If you don't have time for that, a few minutes once a week at a tanning salon will work. Tan with light, not the spray-on method. The light option has harmful UV already removed, and this is far better for you than bathing in chemicals.

Use an exfoliating facial wash before bed. As for the hair most people never see, deal with that also (I use the ¾-inch setting on my buzzer). Use a back brush in the shower with anti-bacterial soap and scrub *EVERYTHING*. If you have any clothes with any holes in them or with other signs of wear and tear (other than jeans), replace them.

You may want to go back and read these paragraphs again to be sure you got all that, and keep in mind that there is a huge difference between grooming and primping. The right amount will attract girls to you while too much will turn you into their best gay friend. It's the difference between cleaned and decorated.

As for buying new clothes, it's time to find shopping help. The most important thing about finding shopping help is to tell that person exactly what statement you want the clothes to make. Remember that you are the final decision-maker, but you are going to pick from what she presents to you. Work with your helper, and don't be afraid to try lots of stuff on. Have fun with it.

You have three options for finding shopping helpers. First, you can ask your gay hair stylist (find one, because no one cuts hair as well as a gay man) if he knows any women who work at a clothing store who could help a terminally straight guy like you get your clothing situation together. Second, ask a woman who finds you sexy if she will go play dress-up with you. Note that the woman has to find you sexy or she will not dress you sexy. Third, go to a clothing store and find a woman working there who you are attracted to and get her help. Simply walk up to her and say, "Excuse me, I'm terminally straight, have no fashion sense, and need new clothes. Please help me!" If she giggles, you found a good one. She will be happy to help you; this is her job. The third option is the best one because you have the type of woman you are interested in dressing you like the type of guy she is interested in. Finally, change it up a few times. After about five different shopping helpers, you should have at least two women you can keep going back to. Their opinions will conflict a little, and this is a good thing. In the end, just go with what you feel is the best choice from all of their options. They are helping you find your personal style. Oh, and one last thing: don't take fashion advice from gay men unless you want to be attractive to gay men.

Style and Fashion

When you meet people, within seconds they have made judgments about who you are based on the way you present yourself. Therefore, you can communicate who you are very quickly through your personal style. This style consists of more than just looking well groomed. We covered that already. I am not going to tell you how I think you should dress, nor do I believe in the idea of fashion dictating what supposedly looks good at any given moment. I think fashion is a bunch of crap. What looks good is always relative. My purpose here is to briefly talk about how to discover and build your own personal style, whatever that may be.

Style is a personal mode of expression. It may or may not adhere to current or prevailing ideals. It may be extreme, or it may be subtle. What is important is that it is distinctive and congruent with who you are. If you're not exactly sure who you are, we will be discussing that in part eight of this book. Style often caters to things such as your musical choice, culture, and lifestyle. It doesn't necessarily fit an existing ideal, because it's not about finding a category that matches your look as much as it's about inspiration that can come from anywhere. Ultimately you want your style to speak about you. It's not about me telling you what looks good. It's about you telling the world who you are. People who have a strong concept of who they are have a strong concept of personal style. It is very important to create a statement of style for yourself. You will then use this statement of style to dictate your choices in clothes, furniture, art, and every aspect involving your personal choice.

My statement of style is as follows:

If it's not simple, clean, comfortable, and amusing, it's not part of my life.

I am a hedonist. I enjoy fine art. I have no houseplants or pets, but I always have fresh-cut flowers in a black vase.

How can a man not be totally enthralled and in awe of the female form? This is my preoccupation, my curse, and my reason for living.

I don't watch sports on TV. It doesn't interest me. I feel guilty if I miss a day in the gym, so I don't.

I'm high maintenance and enjoy it when girls take care of me, which happens frequently.

Straight, sharp lines and edges. Sterile and minimalistic. Carbon fiber, glass, stainless steel, granite, satin, and leather. Plastic should be used only if no other options are available. Black as the

*primary color with silver and gray. The occasional
use of bold primary colors such as red or blue, but
only where unnecessary and unexpected to liven
things up. I despise the natural look of wood and
the color brown.*

*I find most people's concept of perfection to be
limited by their imagination and skill.*

Taking and Marking Space

Let's now build on the concepts of environment we talked about previously. Like lions fighting over territory and resources in the wild, so too are humans continuously playing a game to claim space. The primitive driving force that existed 40,000 years ago that had different tribes throwing spears at each other over hunting grounds still exists in us today. People are still territorial. Even with our destructive, overly politically correct school system, you don't have to watch children play for very long to see this primitive territorial behavior displayed. Children have a preprogrammed set of rules (from evolution) that dictate what is theirs, what is yours, what they want of others, what they offer to others, and everything that relates to conditions of territory and possessions. We claim space with our bodies and, in our absence, with the markers we leave behind.

If I venture into Suburbia, Anyplace, USA, and peek over a few fences into the backyards, it will not be long before I am greeted by a dog. If the family living there has any self-respect, it will be a big dog. I know that the inside of that fence is the territory of that dog. The dog knows this also. If I jump over that fence, the environment becomes shared, and within seconds a fight for that environment will occur. How would the dog mark this territory if he were not there? He would pee on everything.

Possession is nine-tenths of the law. If I am holding something, people tend to believe that it's mine. Therefore, if I am waiting at the airport for a plane, and I am sitting in a public seat at the terminal, that seat is mine. If I leave the seat momentarily to go to the bathroom, but leave some of my possessions on it, such as my coat, it's still mine. All of these little globally accepted social rules are from thousands of years ago, created by our ancestors and still in use today. Personal objects mark personal space and imply territory. This is why a dog will pee on a tree. This is why a husband puts a ring on his wife's finger. This is why Donald Trump puts his name on the top of his buildings. This is why the last time you had your oil changed, the place that did it put a little sticker in the top left corner of your windshield to suggest that the car will be coming back to them in 3,000 miles. This is why the last advertising company you met with left three pens and a coffee cup in your office, all with their name on it. This is why every country has a flag. We leave markers behind stating that this territory belongs to someone.

I've never been one to wear jewelry. I don't even wear a watch. I don't see the point. I can read the time on my cell phone. I'm a minimalist. It's a shame, because if I were the type to wear rings I would steal the following trick from a friend of mine. This guy buys rings in bulk online for cheap. They cost him a few dollars each, but look like something you would pay about $60.00 for. Whenever he goes out to a nightclub, he puts one on. More times than not, the story goes something like this:

> *He meets a cute girl, seduces her, gets her phone number, and before saying goodbye, he uses the power of the ring. As he is saying goodbye, he asks her in a matter-of-fact way if she is a thief. She will giggle a little or give him a confused look and say no while asking why. He will then give her the ring off of his finger, usually putting it on her thumb. As he does, he will tell her to give it back to him next time they see each other. He will tell her that the ring is "special," and he will explain why when he gets it back. He will then give her a little kiss and disappear. The next time they see each other, she will ask why the ring is special, and he will answer, "Simply because it brought you back to me."*

The social equation behind this is brilliant. In fact, it worked too well on many occasions, turning girls into psycho stalkers. I have known many marketing people to use variations of this same powerful concept. Does this guy lose rings? More times than not, no. Every time the girl looks at the ring, she thinks of him, and feels a need to see him again.

Here is another example:

I have a client who is a professional negotiator. He is interesting to watch because he plays all kinds of "games" as he is doing his thing. One of them is turning the boardroom table into a game over physical space and territory. The first thing he will do, depending on the size of the company, is attempt to sit at the head of the table. He will do this only if he is sure he will not offend the other people at the table. He reads clues given when he greets them to tell if he can get away with it or not. The part that really amuses me, however, is that by the end of the negotiation, his laptop bag and briefcase are empty. He puts everything on the table to take up as much space as possible. He brings things that he will never even use such as pads of paper and pens for everyone else with his name on them. When the first person coughs, a bag of cough drops ends up on the table. How thoughtful of him. He takes up more space on the table and he did something for them, so they feel he is a nice guy with their best interests in mind; they owe him. It's a beautiful thing, that bastard. The entire time he is doing this, his arms are at the 10:00 and 2:00 positions taking up twice as much

*space as everyone else at the table and giving him
the appearance of being "open."*

It's never taking up space that will get you into
trouble; it's how you take up the space. Remember that
perception is reality. Have you ever looked at a dog
while he was peeing on a tree? If the dog looked back
at you, it was with a matter-of-fact look like, "Yes, I am
a dog, and I am peeing on a tree. This is my thing: it's
what I do." If in either example above the seducer or
the negotiator had appeared to be uncomfortable or
incongruent, the red flag of manipulation would have
been raised. Both the seducer and the negotiator,
however, do this naturally, just like a dog peeing on a
tree. How you claim space and move things around is a
matter of body language.

By default, Alphas claim space. By default, they
mark that space to deter others from trying to claim it.
Without being completely disrespectful, you should
always be testing and playing the game of "how much
space can I claim?" If you take up too much space in a
public place, such as an armrest at a movie theater, and
piss someone off, simply apologize by saying, "Sorry,
here, let me give you some of my space." Remember
the power of presuppositions (Part 1 – Linguistics), and
you will recognize the power in that statement. In some
situations, this game of seeing what you can get away

with may more closely resemble going over to a friend's house, grabbing a beer from his refrigerator, and taking his favorite seat on his couch. You can always move into another seat. Remember that in situations involving true love, justice, or a big paycheck, be prepared for war. Read *The Art of War* by Sun Tzu.

Touching

Alphas touch a lot. This is normal (just like a dog peeing on a tree). What is a normal amount of touching during normal conversation with anyone? Normal is when you do not go out of your way to touch. Never do it with an expectation or underlying intent; stay neutral. It also means that if someone gives you a normal conversational touch, you do not freak out or run away; you stay neutral. When you touch people, you need to be as comfortable patting them on the shoulder as you are shaking their hand. If you find the last statement untrue for you, it is because you have had more practice shaking hands than you have had occasionally touching as part of normal communication. It's time to desensitize yourself by doing it. Touching is quite literally "connecting" with someone.

There was some debate among my students as to whether touching strangers in the first three seconds of the interaction with them helped or hurt the outcome of that interaction. Most students believed that "poking" at people you do not know makes them uncomfortable and defensive. They believed this from their personal experience. However, some of my students saw me approach women I did not know by simply walking up behind them (unseen), placing my hand on the small of their back, and greeting them with a smile and a few words as they turned.

The answer to this question is all in how it is done, and this is why touching is so powerful. If the average guy approaches an attractive woman unseen from behind, and the first thing he does is touch her, she will freak out. What my students saw me do was different because of the energy I did it with. I was not nervous, jumpy, or unsure of myself. Part of the reason that kind of thing goes so well for me is that I expect it will, and my body language speaks that. It's normal for me now, but it was something I had to learn. When you add touch to communication, you are giving the people you touch more information, and the result is a quicker decision on their part as to what is really going on. If you are uncomfortable when you touch someone, all you communicate to her, and very quickly I may add, is your discomfort.

As you practice and become comfortable with touching people, you will communicate your comfort to them very quickly. I realize that I am basically telling you that you will make a few people uncomfortable as you learn this. This may be true, but only if you go too far too fast. Otherwise, it's minimal. The trick is to start slowly and don't go too far out of your comfort zone. As the weeks go on, keep progressing by going a little more out of your comfort zone. Keep on pushing just a little further every time. Once you have made it through the learning period, take it down a notch, and you will get an amazing response from people. They will tell others that from the first time they met you, you had this incredible energy.

So here are some tips to get you started. The first part is what I call the "What changed?" rule of social interaction. If someone has been working at the same office for the past year, has never touched anyone in any way, and one day walks in as Mr. Touchy-Feely (the extreme opposite), he will have everyone asking what changed, and people will get uncomfortable. However, if this guy changes jobs and regularly uses normal conversational touching right from the get-go at his new job, what changed? Nothing. This is just how the new guy is. The key is to be consistent rather than on-again/off-again with your touching. When changing things in an old environment, you must do it slowly over time. When you are in a mixed group of guys and girls, be sure to touch the guys a little also (think pat on the back, high five, etc.). When you touch girls, be consistent and treat every girl the same. If, when you are with a bunch of married girls, a single girl walks into the room and you are touching only the single girl when you talk, that's bad. In that case, the married girls will ask themselves, "What changed?" They will already know the answer. You are doing it because she is unmarried, and you're gunning for her.

One of the big mistakes I have become aware of is looking at your hand when you touch women. Not only does this draw attention to what you are doing, but somehow it comes across as if you are questioning if touching is OK. If you are looking at what you are doing, you are being cautious. Whenever possible, look women in the eyes (unless, from the position you are in, you cannot see their eyes as is the case when hugging).

A few options if someone says something to you about how often you casually touch:

Them: Well, aren't you the touchy-feely type? (Said as a positive.)

You: Yes, yes I am. (Immediately go back to what you were saying as you touched them.)

Or if they say it as a bad thing:

Them: Well, aren't you a touchy-feely type? (Said as a negative.)

You: Yes, yes I am. I grew up in a very happy, loving family. (Go back to what you were saying.)

Basically the trick is not to miss a beat, because this is normal for you.

So how much is too much? This is a matter of context and then a matter of escalation. Everyone is different and therefore comfortable with different levels. More importantly, those levels change depending on their mood at any given time. Additionally, different things are acceptable in different contexts.

In formal settings, such as at work, the occasional high five, congratulatory pat on the back, or tap/hand on the shoulder (for one second) as you turn your attention to someone is fine and is where it should stop.

In informal settings, we venture into the territory of testing and adjusting. It is simpler than you may think as long as you pay attention. Start off as above, with the small stuff. Do it right away and without hesitation. Then as you slowly progress, pay attention to people's reactions, as in the example below:

> *If I am at a bar and put my hand on a girl's shoulder (for a second) as I meet her, I pay attention to how she responds. If she pulls away when I do it, I know she is not comfortable. I wait, talk more, and build more comfort before I try it again. If she stays neutral or, better yet, shifts her body and attention toward me, she is comfortable. If I then tell a joke and she touches me as she laughs, I have a green light to go further. Five minutes later, when she says something funny, I*

may give her a little hug from the side and tell her she amuses me. To that she will either pull away (she was uncomfortable, so I back off), stay neutral (things are fine, she is comfortable), or lean into the hug (she likes it). This will continue until one of the following three things happens:

1) I remove my attention from her.

2) She removes her attention from me.

3) Things get sexual. If time and/or environment do not allow the actual act, we exchange information to continue the adventure at a later time.

I should probably also mention that most of the time I do stuff like this, I'm not at a bar. I am at the grocery store, or the gym, or buying new socks. This behavior isn't something I "do" on occasion; it's who I "am," so I'm always doing it.

The equation is indeed that simple. The confusing part of this equation is decoding the other people's body language to determine whether they are comfortable, and how to react in either situation. That is what we will talk about next.

Toward and Away Body Language

Toward body language demonstrates that a person is open, comfortable, accepting, agreeing, and paying attention. *Away* body language demonstrates that a person is closed, uncomfortable, refusing, disagreeing, and focused somewhere else. Evolution has built us to move toward things we want or find pleasing and move away from or take a defensive position against things we are scared of or find displeasing.

What if you start a conversation with a girl and she continues to stand there, neither leaning in or away? If you observe neutrality, assume everything is fine. Think of it like this: if someone puts a hundred dollar bill in front of me and tells me that I can have it, I may not grab it instantly, but if someone flings monkey poop in my face, I will start cleaning it off right away. In the same way, it may take her a minute to figure out she likes you. If she doesn't, she is already gone.

As for your body language, always start off from a position of neutrality. One of the biggest mistakes guys make when approaching attractive women is walking straight up to them (head-on) and leaning in as they start talking. It's just too obvious how needy they are. It's the same thing when you sit down to a negotiation in the boardroom. Start from neutral, and if you are in uncharted territory, don't let your body tell them this. Never immediately give 100% of your attention to the person who is expecting 100% of your attention. It is much safer to start off by paying attention to the people who aren't sure if they will be getting your attention. By playing the first minute of the interaction like this, you will win over the betas of the other group and make the most alpha of the other group work a little for your attention.

One of the interesting remnants of evolution is the defensive physical position people take when they are nervous. For example, when someone throws something at your face, your hands go up to protect yourself. This reflex is fun to watch at bars. Girls do it with their purses, and guys do it with their drinks. Girls will use a purse to mark a physical boundary they don't want you to pass, like a shield to protect them. I can tell how comfortable a guy is as he approaches a woman by how high he holds his drink, like a shield to protect him. What's amusing is that this body language doesn't actually do anything to protect them, but it does tell everyone how uncomfortable they are.

Another great indicator of interest or discomfort is foot position. One of the best ways to see this in action is to go to a restaurant with a quiet male friend. When you get a young and attractive waitress, flirt with her. As she becomes more and more attracted, notice the position of her feet as she walks up to the table each time. They will point less toward your friend and more toward you. If, however, you become creepy or weird in your pursuit, her feet will start to point more toward your "safe" friend. This holds true in any combination of social or business interaction. Just remember that if their feet are pointed away, it's either because they are more attracted to someone else, or worse, their body has already started to plan its escape from the discomfort you are inflicting on them. When their feet point in your direction, you have their attention.

As an Alpha, you must learn to reward people's good behavior with your attention and punish their bad behavior by removing your attention. Most people do the opposite when it comes to the body language they display. It's human nature, and I see it in every negotiation and at every bar. Your boss gets distracted and you start leaning toward him. Wrong answer! The girl you met 30 seconds ago at the bar starts leaning away from you and you start leaning in. Wrong answer! Here is how it needs to be done. When they do something good, you move toward them as a reward. When they do something you do not like, you punish by withdrawing your attention. Here is an example from the fountains of the Bellagio in Las Vegas:

> *I'm with an incredibly fun and gorgeous girl I met an hour ago on the Las Vegas Strip. We are waiting for the next water show in front of the Bellagio Hotel. I have my arm around her as a*

*bold guy on the other side of her tries to strike up a
conversation with her. At first, I ignore it. After
45 seconds of them talking, I remove my arm from
her. After another 15 seconds, my body isn't
touching her anymore, and I've started to talk to a
girl on my other side. Instantly, the original girl
turns away from the other guy and puts her arm
around me. I reward her by blowing off the girl I
just started talking to and putting my arm back
around the original girl.*

When they're good, you use *towards body
language*. When they're bad, you use *away body
language*. Just remember that if they are pulling away
and you respond by pulling away, they will not
reengage with you unless they perceive value in you. If
they pull away and you chase, they will perceive an
even lower value of you. This game is won when they
perceive you have high value, you never chase, and you
have no problem with removing your attention when
they do something you don't like.

Don't be oversensitive when you read the body
language of others. Keep in mind that sometimes
movements that others make have nothing to do with
you or what you are saying. It can be dangerous to read
too much into any one thing. People who are good at
reading body language base the read on multiple

movements and pay attention to what they all say combined. It could be possible that you didn't make her nervous and she really did just need to go to the bathroom. She might be leaning to the right because she has a bruise on her left ass cheek from rollerblading yesterday. You will never be sure of the reason for one specific movement, but when you take everything into account, you will know what's up.

Dynamics

Every interaction, moment by moment, will display one of three combinations of toward and away body language. The first is *toward/toward*. This combination is what we see between two newlyweds on their honeymoon, a mother and her baby, a masseuse and her client. The second is *away/away*. This combination can be seen when both people lose interest in each other and simply walk away. The third and most common is *toward/away*. The best example of this combination would be a man walking on a busy street with a hundred dollar bill attached to the back of his shirt. People will pursue him as he walks away from them. The thing that needs to be understood about toward/away is how human psychology sets this dynamic up:

> *There was an interesting university study done that involved 10 girls, 10 guys, and 20 cards numbered 1–20. Guys were given the odd-numbered cards, girls the even. Each person, without seeing his or her number, attached the card to a hat he or she was wearing so everyone else could see it. The students were then told to pair up with the highest number they could. What happened? Everyone figured out the value of his or her card very quickly. The girl with the 20*

figured out she had the highest number when every guy in the room walked toward her at the same time. The guy with the 1 figured it out when no one walked up to him until the end when everyone else was paired up and the girl with the 2 approached him. When the experiment was over, everyone was perfectly paired up sequentially.

Looking Comfortable from Being Comfortable

Just how comfortable do you want to look? It's not a matter of "looking" comfortable so much as it is a matter of being comfortable. If the fire alarm went off, you would be the last person to get out of your chair simply because you are so comfortable and reclined back into it. An uncomfortable man who senses danger will sit on the edge of his seat, enabling a fast getaway. Whenever I am at a bar or nightclub, I will position myself in one of three ways after starting a conversation with someone:

> *Leaning away, slouching back in a chair; leaning away with my back against the wall; or my favorite, leaning away with my back resting on the bar. If I am talking with an attractive young lady, it looks to everyone as though she is seducing me. What does she feel? Well, definitely not that I am the one chasing her.*

Keep in mind that people tend to run when chased. People are most attracted to what they cannot have. If someone is trying to get your approval or validation, you already have theirs.

Mastery

When you were a child, you had to learn to "bite your tongue" and not say everything that you were thinking. Similarly, you must learn to control your body language. You cannot let your body say everything that goes through your mind. After you have become aware, have found neutrality, and are comfortable, you must then learn control. Only time can teach you control. With practice, you will know when to chase, run, hold your ground, or throw mixed signals, and when to simply be fluid. You will be able to control what emotions your body speaks and know when to speak them. Ultimately your props, body language, paralinguistics, and linguistics will all be in harmony, and the rewards for that are immense. The effects you will have on those around you will be nothing short of incredible.

Power Communication Part 4
Eye Contact

Week 4

Do you believe in love at first sight? It seems a direct connection exists between the eyes and the heart that reason and logic know nothing of. Why do people say that "seeing is believing" but never say this about any of our other four senses? The eyes have something that the other senses don't. Have you ever talked with someone who you felt could "see right through you?" We all have. Why is it that the eyes are often referred to as "the window to the soul?" Why do we feel naked when we stare into each other's eyes? You are about to gain, understand, and learn control of this force.

Eye contact is not the same as staring. People hate the "zoned-out" look of a stare. If two people are having a conversation and one of them keeps staring at a blemish on the other's face, discomfort results for the person with the blemish. If you and I are having a conversation and I keep staring at the tops of your ears (switching from ear to ear every few seconds and looking at nothing else), it will not be long before your concentration breaks. Try to weird out a friend with this sometime.

Staring is holding your gaze at something. Eye contact is looking directly into the other person's pupils. Accomplishing this is simple in concept yet surprisingly difficult in action. Here is how it is done. You look directly into the black centers of the other person's eye. Not the eyelashes, not the white part, not the colored part, but directly at the black center. Now forget that the rest of the world exists for a moment. Hold this without blinking until the color of the other person's eyes registers in your peripheral vision AND you have finished saying the color to yourself in your head. Do this as soon as each person gets close enough for you to figure it out. Just keep on looking at their eyes as they approach until you have fulfilled the task. As you get more comfortable, add a descriptor word in front of the color as you say it to yourself. The last person I spoke with had "bright green," and the person before that had "ice blue." The cop who pulled me over yesterday had "speckled hazel" and did not write me a speeding ticket (not a coincidence). If you just can't stand it for the first few days you are learning this, you can cheat by moving your focus from pupil to pupil, but you must be looking at only the black center of the other person's eyes – **NOTHING ELSE** – until you have silently decided on the descriptor and color in your head. As a side note, when people switch their gaze back and forth between the other person's pupils, it signifies that they are working to figure the other person out. As you get better, focus only on their pupil to your right as you play this game.

Direct eye contact has a very powerful effect on the amygdala. This part of the brain plays a primary role in the processing and memory of emotional reactions. Scientists who were recording cell responses in the amygdala as it was fed information by the visual centers, found that different cells fire in response to the direction of someone else's eye gaze toward you. One group of cells fires for a direct gaze, aimed directly into the center of the pupil. If someone looks slightly up, down, left, right, or any other position slightly outside of the center of the pupil, a different group fires for each. The amygdala also knows if the right or left eye is being directly gazed into and fires a different group for each eye. With eye contact, the other person's brain knows exactly how you are looking at him or her, and the slightest change makes huge differences in the emotions processed in relation to you.

Alphas who have mastered eye contact get the attention of people the fastest and hold it the longest. They connect with people quickly and more completely. They also come across as the most confident and most trustworthy. The more they practice, the easier it gets because they are focusing their attention completely on the other person. Its impossible to be self-conscious when you are 100%

focused on the other person. Remember this when practicing. The more completely you pay attention to the other person, the easier it gets and the more power you gain. Forcing the focus of your eyes is focusing your attention. Focus completely and you will completely forget about your own ego.

For the person being looked at, this type of eye contact sends a very powerful message. For some people, you will be the only person that day who will truly look at them and truly see them. The effect can be one of simple acknowledgment or can create a feeling of instant empathy. This simple look can wake people up as they sleepwalk through their day. Some people may make eye contact with a hundred strangers in a day, but it's the Alpha's eye contact that they will remember for the remainder of the week, all without even speaking to them.

I remember the day the above concept took hold of my brain:

I was on a crowded sidewalk in New York. Like getting hit by a lightning bolt, I had an epiphany. I was looking at the people around me the same way I was looking at the sidewalk, light posts, and street signs. How could I possibly expect strangers to be warm to me when I looked at them the same way I was looking at inanimate, lifeless objects?

After this epiphany, I upped the ante of the game. In addition to describing the color of their eyes, I would search out their eyes for emotion. I discovered more times than not, I would find whatever emotion I was looking for. For this very important reason, I learned to look for only the good in people's eyes. Please clearly understand the danger I'm warning you of here. Staring into the eyes of gang members in South Central Los Angeles and seeing anger/hate will put you in a dangerous place. Seek the good in people, because that's what you want to interact with.

As my skills progressed, I would search their eyes out, hold the look for two seconds, blink once, and continue to look straight into their soul for an additional two seconds. In my head, I was saying, "Lean back and relax. Look them straight in the eyes. Calming oceans of deep blue. One-one-thousand, two-one-thousand, blink, one-one-thousand, two-one-thousand." It seemed like an eternity. I would talk with people who did not know me, but somehow within a few seconds, they felt they did know me. It worked every time. I slowed them down, I calmed them, and I used my eyes to interrupt the indifference of their routine behavior. It wasn't aggression; it was registering my presence, my acknowledgment of them as a real person, and our mutual transparency. It was powerful, very powerful. People who I had never spoken to before were my friends; drinks magically became free, business became easier, and I could get women to approach me without even saying a word. The best part was getting discounts that I neither deserved nor asked for from people standing behind cash registers.

Once I got this down, I didn't have to think about it or do it mechanically anymore. It became automatic. Things for me now are even stranger. A day doesn't go by without someone asking where we have met before, even though we never have. My favorite is when a girl zones out for a second and then says something like, "Sorry, déjà-vu." That one always gets a smile out of me, especially when she's hot.

Learned Through Martial Arts

One of the many lessons I learned in the martial arts community is to never take your eyes off of someone within striking distance. When we bow at each other, we always hold eye contact. The same is true when you shake someone's hand. Do not look down; always maintain eye contact. Looking anywhere but in the eyes as you bow or shake hands is not just physically dangerous, it's submissive. Go too far in the other direction, however, and you become aggressive with your eye contact. The easier time you have looking into other people's eyes, the harder time they will have looking into yours. This is just how the balance of power plays out, at least in the beginning. As your skills grow, your self-confidence will lead you to abandon fears, and with that, aggression disappears. You become centered and transparent. This is the point when strangers will actually feel more comfortable looking into your eyes. Just remember that possessing any kind of power tends to make those around you unsettled as you inevitably trigger their primal fight-or-flight response. It's the self-control of that power that allows them to relax and enjoy being around it.

In my early twenties, between the gym and the dojo, I was spending four hours per day working out (I was kickboxing competitively). Not only did

I look like I could effortlessly destroy people, but it was a matter of fact. It took some getting used to. Learning what I did about eye contact on top of that made me a freak of nature, yet somehow I've never been in a fight outside of the ring. Some people can handle power, while others can't. Don't be a bully as you learn this.

Blinking

One of the things people do to mask the breaking of eye contact is to blink. If I am talking to a girl and notice that she is blinking more than the normal 12–15 times per minute, there is a good chance that her emotions are running away with her. She likes me. She blinks more to break and control the emotional connection our eye contact is creating.

This is where the staring contest came from. The longer you can hold a gaze into people's eyes, the more power you have over them. Keep in mind that people know there is a physical need to lubricate the eyes, and if you never blinked, you would freak people out. The following is a list of things that will increase lubrication and decrease your blink rate.

Drink less alcohol. It dries your eyes out.

Eat more omega-3 fatty acids. They increase the effectiveness of each blink.

Wear glasses to block the wind that can dry out your eyes.

Choose glasses, because LASIK eye surgery and contact lenses tend to dry your eyes out.

Move your eyes less, because the more they move, the more lubrication they need.

Keep bright light behind you. The brighter the light is, the more it will strain your eyes.

Put pressure on the tear ducts (right behind your lashes). This pushes out more lubricant before your next stare-down.

Your goal is about 8 to 10 blinks a minute on average. Less than that and you are trying too hard. It's not close to normal, and you will just look weird.

Pupil Dilation and Emotion

People's pupils will grow and shrink in response to their mood, focal point, and current mental processes. The pupils become large when the person is attracted or pleased and shrink when repelled or displeased. It is very important to note that these changes are in comparison to whatever the normal state is for the amount of light present in any situation. The other factor that makes the pupils grow and shrink is the amount of ambient light. When it is bright, the pupils shrink to avoid too much light. When it is dark, they grow to let more available light in. As you become comfortable always looking into the pupils, you will develop a sense for what is normal in different amounts of light. Also, keep in mind that drugs and alcohol can completely tweak pupil size and screw all of this up.

Unconsciously people notice the relative sizes of other people's pupils. When people see dilated pupils, they unconsciously know that the other person is in a heightened positive emotional state. The most interesting thing is that in response to seeing this, they tend to enter a heightened positive emotional state also. In other words, when people see large pupils, their emotional state is influenced, and they tend to go along for the ride. In the game of eye contact, if you are attracted to those around you, those around you tend to become attracted to you.

A study was done with pictures that had been digitally altered to adjust pupil size. Participants viewed pictures of strangers. Every stranger had three identical pictures in the set. Two pictures were untouched, and one was digitally altered to enlarge pupil size. The participants consistently choose the altered images, those with dilated pupils, as the most attractive. When asked the reason for their choices, they did not even notice the differences in pupil size; it all happened on the unconscious level.

People with dilated pupils are focusing on internal emotional experiences. They may be imagining, visualizing, thinking about the past, guessing about the future, remembering a smell or taste, wondering what sex with you would be like, or attempting to search out your emotions. They appear dreamy, nonthreatening, and sensitive. When people see someone in this state, they tend to fall into the same state.

Forcing Pupil Dilation

Because pupil dilation builds such strong, deep rapport, it can become a very powerful tool. Forcing your pupils to dilate can lead people you are talking with into a very advantageous state for you. They become putty in your hands. This is why women used to drop belladonna into their eyes, which would cause pupil dilation. The result was "bedroom eyes," and the result of that was amped-up attraction from the men they looked at. (Don't try it yourself. Belladonna has since been proven to be harmful to the eyes.)

So how do you force pupil dilation to build an emotional connection? The first step is to hold eye contact with someone you are attracted to. If you want to turbocharge it from there, you need to blur the field of vision the other person is in, causing your pupils to dilate. To learn how to do this, practice by looking at an object about 25 feet away. While keeping your focus on the object, take your index finger, point it up, and slowly move it from your side into your field of vision until it's right in front of the object. If you keep your focus on the far object, you will see two fingers (double vision). Next, practice doing the same thing on an object you are already looking at. When you can do that, you've got it. All you need to do is start seeing the person's face with double vision, just as you had seen your finger, and your eyes will automatically start dilating. When you do this to people during emotional conversations, you will feel the energy of the interaction change as you draw them in.

The most interesting thing I discovered while mastering this is what I call the *failsafe feedback loop*. It's nature's way of keeping you honest with this technique, and it makes me giggle. Here is how it works:

> *If I am with a girl who I'm only slightly attracted to and use this, a very interesting thing happens. By dilating my eyes while I tell her what she wants to hear, her eyes dilate as it works. Because this only works while maintaining eye contact, I get sucked into the emotional loop I just created as I see her eyes dilate. Suddenly I'm falling for her. Starting this feedback loop is like starting a food fight. You don't stay unaffected for very long.*

Bright Eyes and Dark Eyes

You have an advantage if you have blue or green eyes. The brighter the color is surrounding the pupil, the easier it is to notice dilation. Because people with light eyes are easier to read emotionally, people tend to trust them more. This is why people tend to gravitate toward sexual partners (if all other factors are the same) with light eyes, because they want to know how someone they are attracted to is feeling about them. This is also why most people have dark eyes, because from an evolutionary standpoint, keeping others guessing about your emotions is an asset allowing for deception. If you are like me and happen to have color-changing blue/green eyes that tend to look blue when you wear blue and green when you wear green, the force will be strong with you. Yours is a game of emotional transparency, with the added bonus of variation to keep things interesting. If you have dark eyes, play up being mysterious because it makes you harder to read.

Communicating Expectations

Evolution has programmed us to look away from disaster. The saying is, "I can't even watch." It's what cowering is all about: looking away. When "the shit is about to hit the fan," most people "put their head in the sand." You are going to have to learn to get past that, as this next story illustrates:

When I was younger, I played ice hockey. I was a goaltender. The first thing I had to learn was to keep my eyes open. The natural reaction for any normal person is to close his eyes in defense when a loud slapping sound sends a ¾-pound piece of vulcanized rubber at his head from 40 feet away at a speed of 90-plus miles an hour. It was a rush, and I loved it. The next big hurdle I had to overcome was to modify my built-in "get the hell out of the way" response evolution blessed me with. Ultimately a goaltender needs to reprogram his brain to jump in front of danger and keep his eyes open, all without thinking about it as he plays in a world timed by fractions of a second. Oh, and it's not just the puck, but also the 220-pound guys skating at him at full speed. When a player skates toward the goal, what does the non-blinking eye contact of the goaltender communicate? It says, "I

know exactly what I am doing. You're not a threat.
I own this moment."

This is what you want to communicate with your eyes in a business negotiation. The statement is that you have opened your awareness, and nothing is going to get by you. You communicate an expectation that they will either comply or you will be able to navigate any resistance. This is not aggression, but rather full awareness in the moment.

Power Communication Part 5
Questions vs. Statements

Week 5

Everyone, including you, prefers to receive rather than to give. However, it is far more beneficial for you to give than receive. When it comes to the structure of communication, giving vs. receiving is defined by questions vs. statements. Every question involves asking someone for something: you are asking for information. By contrast, a statement involves giving someone something: you are giving information.

Please keep in mind that I am **<u>not</u>** talking about the decision of what to communicate and what not to communicate. Nor am I advocating full and total disclosure instantly or in every situation. What I am talking about is *how* you communicate something after you decide to do so. Information is power. Do not blindly give away your power. There is a basic rule of negotiation stating that the first person to say what they want loses. This rule holds very true. What you are going to learn here is how to disguise questions as statements and why you want to do so whenever possible.

Defense Default

Society has conditioned us to have an automatic default response of "no" when we are asked a question. This conditioning starts when we are young children. Consider small children who have just started walking and are getting into everything around the home. Any time the children get into something they shouldn't, one of their parents says "no." However, when the children are doing something perfectly acceptable in their exploration, they usually hear silence rather than the word *yes*. I find it very interesting that, as children, we hear the word *no* an exponentially greater number of times than the word *yes*. My next example shows the state this leaves us in as adults.

Consider a stranger walking up to you and saying, "Can I ask you a question?" Never ask people if you can ask them something. Remember that the default answer will be no, and you are just being redundant by asking if you can ask something. You just did. You never need permission to talk to people. You just talk to them, but remember that they are not obligated to respond, even though most people feel they are.

Now consider that same stranger skipping the question about the question and just asking his *question. The stranger walks up to you and starts talking. He says, "Can I..." (at this point you already have your default answer of no ready to go) "...give you $100.00?" You say, "OK." Silly you. That's perfectly fine. Why did you assume it would be something bad for you to say yes to? Social programming, that's why.*

If the stranger would simply walk up to you and say, "Here is $100.00 for no reason. Have a nice day!" We may wonder if he is crazy, but your defenses wouldn't go up. Defenses go up only when we start to wonder what the other person wants from us.

Remember that the easiest way to get past people's defenses is never to put them in a defensive position. Avoid the defense default of "no" for questions by phrasing them as statements.

Familiarity

Strangers talk in questions. Friends talk in statements. For most of us, when we met new people, we try to figure them out to adjust our personality to fit theirs. Not only do we betray who we truly are when we do this, but more importantly, it's very boring. Relationships come together on similarities, but it's the differences that keep them together, and more importantly, keep them interesting.

Consider two men meeting. They are both in the oil industry. One man owns oil fields, and the other owns a company that manufactures oil barrels. Similar yet different equals a great relationship.

You do not have to be the same. Just behave as if you already know each other. Don't focus on the contents of the statements so much as making the statements. Below is a conversational example for someone you just met.

Oh, you're Janet. We were just about to walk across the street to the sushi place, or maybe the Mexican place. Are you hungry? Do you like sushi? Would you like to come along? Mexican would be OK, unless you want sushi.

The correct way to "ask" Janet to join you is:

Hello, Janet. Carrie and I are on our way to enjoy sushi across the street. You look like someone who knows how to use chopsticks. (Half-second pause) This way then.

Will this work 100% of the time? No, and neither will any question, but the second option has a far better likelihood of success with someone you just met. The human brain is simply the most incredible mechanism in the known universe for recognizing patterns. When you meet new people, the more you talk in statements, the more they will feel as if they have known you for longer than they have. The pattern is that statements translate to familiarity.

Invitation or Invasion

A question says, "I want to get into your world." A statement says, "You are invited into my world." If I ask if I may enter your world and you say no, that is far worse than if I invite you into my world and you do not join. Wanting to enter yours implies that yours is better. An invitation to enter mine implies mine is better. If my invitation is turned down, I can be of the opinion that you do not know what you are missing.

Seeding Questions with Statements

If you have to ask a question (as you often will in ordinary conversation), use a statement before the question. Think of it as giving someone something before asking for something. The statement should say something about your opinion or intent, as this next example shows.

> *Cindy, I love the way your glasses fit your face so perfectly. I have got to know, did you have that style in mind when you were shopping for them, or was it more like you were just trying everything on and when you put those on you were surprised to look up and see how perfect they were on you?*

The trick, as you see above, is to give more information than you are asking for. The same thing can be done at the office. Consider the differences between the following:

> *Cindy, will you have the TPS reports done by 4:30?*

> *Cindy, I have a meeting at 4:30 today that I will need the TPS reports for. Will they be done by then?*

In the bottom example, we tell Cindy why the question is important before we even ask the question, and this changes how Cindy will answer. As you practice this, you will see that you get answers closer to what you desire if you make a statement before the question to guide the answer.

How to Guess Correctly

At one point in my life I became fascinated with people who do fortune-telling. Now keep in mind that I do not believe in anything that is not scientifically provable. I figured that there was some kind of trick to it, similar to a magician's act. I wanted to learn the trick. Logic told me that if I could "read the minds" of my clients, profits would no less than double. Additionally, I thought that if I could "read the minds" of the women I dated, I might actually be able to answer the age-old question of what women want.

This quest became an obsession. At great expense and difficulty, I finally found a wise man who was willing to teach me the art. I was correct on two things. The first was that there was no hocus-pocus to it. It was indeed a system. The second was that it was very powerful. While the specifics are outside the scope of this book (I will fully disclose it in a future book), I will talk to you briefly about what to do when you make the wrong statement.

Whenever your statement is a guess, watch the body language of the person you are talking with for the answer as you make the statement. Remember from part three of this book that untrained people aren't even aware that their body language is constantly saying things. Look for the small cues that tell you if they agree (toward movement) or disagree (away movement) with your statement. As you build your statement, all you need to remember is that if their body language starts to say no, you use the word *but* in your sentence to start saying the opposite. Remember from part one of this book that the word *but* is a destroyer that works to nullify everything in the sentence preceding it. Read their body language quickly so you can shape your statements in real time. If you avoid absolutes and keep practicing, you'll get better results than you'd expect. Practice in social settings and move it into business as you become better at it. As you get better, more and more of your statements will appear to be correct. Get good enough at it, and if you ever lose your job, you'll be able to find work as a fortune-teller. Master it, and you'll always have work in whichever profession you choose.

Below are two normal conversational examples from someone who's mastered this game:

Jason, I can see that a big factor in your decision on this deal may be overall value (Jason squints his eyes slightly and pulls his head away one inch), **but** *the greater issue will be quality. (He nods his head slightly. I knew if it wasn't value, it was quality as they tend to oppose each other, and now my client feels that I understand him.)*

Linda, I can tell you are ready for adventure (her posture slumps), **but** *tonight we will have a quiet dinner at home, and we will go out for adventure Friday night. (Linda is amazed at how well I can "read her" but in reality I have no idea what is going on in her head until she tells me, subtly with her body language. In reality, I do "understand her" like no other guy she had dated.)*

A look through the pages of any history book will show you that everyone fits into three categories. There are followers, failed leaders, and successful leaders. Followers are always using questions as they ask their leaders what to do next. Failed leaders make the wrong statements, and because of that, people stop listening to them. Successful leaders always seem to make the right statements, and you now understand how that game is played.

Power Communication Part 6
Limited Sensory Communication

Week 6

Over the years of teaching communication skills, I have noticed one common misconception shared by the majority of my students. They seem to believe that a completely different set of rules exists for talking on the telephone, sending email, text messaging, or using any other form of what I call *limited sensory communication*. For communication like this, you have less to work with, so the more you will need to understand what you're doing. It's not that the rules are different; it's that I need to give you a more complete understanding of those rules. You are about to learn some entertaining things about human nature, how things play out over a timeline, and some very important differences between the male and female brain.

Failure Is a Process

Today's results are the product of yesterday's actions. Where you are right now is the product of your thinking and the resulting actions you have taken or not taken in life. Success is a process that involves many steps. Failure is also a process, and it too, involves many steps. Most people have developed a very convenient false belief that success is a long complicated process and that failure is something that just happens. They believe that failure comes out of nowhere, in an instant, for some reason that only "fate" can say for sure.

I remember discovering an interesting pattern many years ago at one of my companies. Removing all of my senses, I could still tell you how well a sales meeting with a customer went simply by the amount of time the salesperson spent telling me the story afterwards. If it went poorly and they just didn't care, it would be a very short story. It would sound something like, "I don't know. It just didn't work." If it went well, much more time would be spent by my staff telling me how awesome their sales skills are, even if a four-year-old could have done the same thing. The longest conversations, however, would be when it went so bad that my staff was trying to cover their asses. This would sound a little like, "It wasn't my fault," and "There was nothing I could have done."

Neither fate nor coincidence exists. Everything in existence works on mathematical models as mathematics is the language of the universe. These mathematical models have rules that keep the universe from self-destructing by maintaining balance. Both success and failure are processes. They are actually at two opposing ends of the same spectrum that describes any given event. In the grand scheme of things, assuming you start in the middle, both require the same number of steps to fully accomplish. So why is that people try to complicate success and simplify failure? Because it feels good. If you believe that success is difficult, you do not feel so bad when you don't achieve it, because it's very difficult. On the rare occasion that you do achieve it, the high of success becomes even better. If you believe that failure is almost unavoidable and easy to fall into no matter what you do, you don't feel so bad when you continually fail.

The point as it relates to phone calls, text messages and email is simply this: if everything seemed to go perfectly during your initial face-to-face interaction but it all falls apart during the first phone call, then everything did not go perfectly during your initial face-to-face interaction. If your marketing campaign was perfect and generated lots of inbound calls, but once the potential customers got on the phone everything fell apart, then your marketing campaign was actually **not** perfect. Nine times out of ten, something went wrong before you even made it to the phone, email, or text message. Retrace your steps, improve on the step prior to where everything went sideways, and your current problems will start to dissolve. Failure is a process, and you are in control of that process.

I hear this one frequently when I coach guys:

I called her and asked her out for Friday night but she said she already had plans.

I always respond with this:

If Brad Pitt would have been asking her out rather than you, what do you think her answer would have been?

Likewise, if Angelina Jolie left me a voicemail message in which she simply said, "Hi Drawk, it's Angelina," farted, and then hung up, guess what? I would call her back.

If the next email I get from Donald Trump starts off with, "Hey, asshole!" I will still feel cool that he sent me a message.

Always ask yourself how much value the person assigned to you before you picked up the phone, typed the email, or sent the text message. If you get your value high enough, neither your choice of communication medium nor content will matter much. Remember the basics. Perceived value is everything.

Limited Senses

Personally, I hate any form of communication that falls short of live one-on-one interaction. It's painful for me. It's sensory deprivation. I have spent years learning how to use my senses to the fullest of human potential. Additionally, when I am communicating with people, I'm hitting every sense they have at both a conscious and unconscious level. For me, talking on the telephone is like telling an NBA player to shoot hoops from a wheelchair, with a broken wheel. It's beyond frustrating. Unfortunately, it's also a necessity. We live in a world that has become extremely productive because of the communication technology we have available. For example, this book you are reading now would not be possible without technology. On the positive side, my message can reach billions but the message is weaker than if I had delivered it to you in person.

Depending on the limits of the technology you are using, you are working with limited information. All of the core rules remain the same, but you have less data going back and forth to work with. The first thing to learn is that the fewer senses involved, the easier it is to turn someone down. Whether it's the girl from the bar or the real estate mogul you met on the golf course, he or she may find it's easiest to give you a phone number and reject you over the phone than to simply reject you in person. It's not your phone skills that are lacking. It's that they do not see you with enough value, and they would rather turn you down when they don't have to see your disappointment.

Lack of One Sense Builds the Others Stronger

It's a fact that people who lose their eyesight develop better hearing. When a person loses one sense, the other four tend to get stronger. Do not use handicapped communication as an excuse for failure. If anything, it is an excuse for learning. When you are talking on the phone, you are focused on practicing your linguistics and paralinguistics. When you are sending a text message, it's all about linguistics. When you are back conversing live, the things you were forced to focus on before will now be stronger. Challenge equals training. Train every opportunity you can.

Time Can Change Everything

One of the factors that can have you questioning your non-face-to-face communication skills is time. Things change. The girl you met last Friday night at the club was out drinking and dancing when you met her. You need to realize that when you call her a few days later, she is no longer in that environment. It may be Tuesday night and she is doing her taxes. She is in a totally different environment, frame of mind, and mood. When you call her, you need to be aware of this disconnect and pull her back into your happy world. Women fall in and out of completely different emotional states very quickly. Guys have a tendency to pick up the conversation from where and when it left off. It is this huge disconnect that leaves guys trying to figure out what they are "doing wrong." The answer is that they are blind to the concept of "speedy emotional disconnect and mood change" in women. To understand this concept enough for practical use, act as if you are talking to a completely different girl every 10 minutes. You will be shocked to discover how well this works.

Similarly, the guy you met at the yacht club, who said you'd be perfect to work with his company, may have just gotten a call from his accounting department informing him of his impending bankruptcy. While he remembers his conversation with you, facts have changed drastically, and he's more upset than a toddler who just dropped his ice cream cone. Landing that job during your first phone call to him will now be next to impossible.

You now understand that time changes emotional state. Connections with people are always changing and require maintenance. You're about to learn how to not only maintain but strengthen those connections, even if you have fewer than all five senses to work with.

The Telephone

Now that you understand the basics, let's cover some specific rules to get you started. Remember, rules are guidelines to the wise and laws to the fool. The more you practice, the more you can bend the guidelines. Remember, it's all about perceived value.

Always show your Caller ID. Don't be the person hiding in the shadows stalking people. People who are in high demand (important business people and social butterflies) do not answer Caller-ID-Blocked calls. The reason is very simple: blocking your Caller ID makes the statement that you believe you have low value with the people you are calling. You are saying, "But if they know it's me, they will not pick up." People who have value show their Caller ID because they know they have value. I show my Caller ID because I know there is a better chance of people answering when they see it's me. Build your value with people first, and then use it to your advantage when you call. And if you are blocking your Caller ID because you don't want them to be able to call you back, you need to ask yourself why. Is this something your staff should be doing for you? Are you doing this out of some kind of fear? It's time to find the real issue and deal with it.

Always leave a message. You do not need to have a complete conversation with someone's voicemail, but always say why you called. If you are asking people to call you back, give them the reason. Do not ever leave the "Hi, it's me. Call me back," message. That message is not only boring but also very disrespectful of someone's time. Busy people manage many return phone calls on any given day. They like to know the sensitivity of the call. Do you need something from them before the close of business New York time today, or are you calling to ask if they are interested in attending a party two days from now? Assume you are important enough to get a return call. People who call multiple times without leaving a message are being reactionary and are lowering their value every time they call and do not leave a message.

Always check the voicemail message before returning the call. Don't be one of these idiots who call back without first listening to the voicemail message. Someone took the time to record the message, so you can certainly take the time to listen to it before calling back. Asking people to repeat themselves because you are lazy is stupid. They may not even need to talk to you because they were just leaving information, and they may no longer have that information in front of them. If they were asking you to take action before calling them back, you just wasted their time with an unnecessary call. Information is power, so collect all the information you can before returning the call.

Use an organizational system. You are an important person with lots going on but you must always remember to call people back and fulfill the obligations you agreed to. Get a modern cell phone with the organizational power of a computer and learn how to use it, or use a torn piece of paper that you always have in your pocket if you must. Whatever works for you is fine, but establish a system and always use it. Disorganized people tend to forget things and never give these things a second thought, so they aren't even aware of how much they forget. My point is that if you're not using an organizational system, you need that system more than you realize. Use it religiously!

When to return calls. You return every call and you do it as quickly as comfortably possible. The only time you do not return a call is after you have told someone in a previous call that you are not interested. Be polite, but be clear and use the word *no*. If that person still keeps calling, you have the option of ignoring the call. I will usually tell people twice before ignoring them. Also, it is perfectly acceptable to call someone back right away and tell them you have only a minute to talk now but wanted to set up a time for a longer conversation later. Don't ignore people because you don't want to give them bad news. You face your problems head-on and call the parties involved quickly to start working on the solution. The only exception to this rule is in times of "war" when giving the enemy time to react would be stupid.

Know the current local time. If you are calling across time zones, know the local time and respect it. The easiest way to figure out the local time somewhere is Google. Just type in "current time in London" or "current time in New York" or "current time in Sydney." This trick will work for just about any decent-sized city in the world.

Know when to disconnect. High-value people know how and when to unplug. I turn my phone off when I sleep, at the movie theater, at important meetings, and during romantic occasions. If you live a life in which others are always interrupting you, you have self-value issues. Developing a simple set of life rules can lead to a good night's sleep in more ways than one.

Do not return phone calls with email. This is incredibly impersonal and disrespectful. It tells people that they have very little value with you. If someone asks you to send directions or pictures, great; use email. However, do not use email just because you do not want to talk on the phone. If you do not like talking with someone on the phone, call that person and talk about why you don't like talking to them on the phone. Do not hide behind your email.

Delegation. If you are going to pawn someone off on someone else, you must still call that person back to explain what you are doing and why. Do not hide behind your staff or personal assistant. The real trick is not to have all these people calling you directly in the first place.

Set a crisis boundary. We have all received those calls either at work or from friends (or worse, family) in which they're in a big huff about whatever tragedy just hit them. They are calling because they "need" your help. Let me start off by saying that I like being able to help people, and I enjoy helping people. The problem is when it becomes a reoccurring theme, because they did not learn the lesson last time. Teach them how to prevent a future occurrence as you help them the first time. If they repeat the same problem twice, ask if they took your advice from last time. If they did not, you will not help them this time. Do not let people use you as an excuse to be stupid repeatedly, just because they know you will rescue them. Do not let people use you as an emotional dumpster on a reoccurring basis. Every relationship has its ups and downs, but over the long haul, it needs to be a positive relationship for everyone involved. Change the relationship or end it.

Don't participate in whining or gossip. It's normal for men to talk about their past, present, and future conquests. It's normal for women to talk about their feelings, hopes, dreams, and aspirations. What is unacceptable is when any of this takes the form of "why people suck" or "how people keep screwing me over." Don't speak it, and don't listen to it.

Obligation builds resentment. One of my life-changing moments happened the day I decided that I would no longer do what I do not want to do. Now don't misunderstand me here. It takes some brains to figure out what I am talking about. You and I must think about how our actions will affect us over the long haul. As an example, I still go to the dentist, not because I like going to the dentist but because I don't want my teeth to rot. I am also not talking about skipping out on your responsibilities. Keep your commitments. What I am talking about here is abolishing the feeling of guilt. I gave up on guilt a long time ago and just don't feel it anymore. Part of this involves making the right decisions in the moment (or the best I can at the time), and the other part is to never ever let anyone use guilt to get me to do something I don't want to do. This holds especially true with family. It enrages me to see people pull the "but I'm family" card, as if you have to put up with someone's bad behavior because you are related to him or her. I don't care who people are; if they are an ongoing source of negativity in your life, remove them from your life if you cannot help them to change their behavior. If you have a hard time figuring this one out, ask yourself the following question: "If this person were not related to me, would I be friends with him or her?" If the answer is no, then work on the relationship. Ultimately if the person is just an unchanging asshole or bitch, remove him or her from your life. Remember, any action done because of an obligation that you did not somehow bring on yourself, and that you are not able to undo, can result only in resentment.

Ease of hanging up. It amazes me that people forget how easy it is to hang up the phone. Now I am not advocating that you just start hanging up on people without warning. That would be rude and not as much fun as my way. Take control! If people cold call you, tell them that you are not interested, and if they keep talking, interrupt them by saying, "I think you are underestimating my ability to hang up on you." If they say anything other than "goodbye" in response to that, hang up. If you pick up any call, you are in control of that call, and this serves as a good warning that if they don't start playing nice, the call is going to end very quickly. I have to admit to using this very line on a former girlfriend. I say former because that's the last time I spoke with her. Hey, what can I say? Go out with a bang!

Email and Text Messages

As a general rule, call people. Never send a message when you can place a phone call. You always want to be as personal as you can be with people. That said, there are some times when an email or text message is better. Text messages work great when you are in a meeting, but keep in mind that if the meeting is important enough to not step out to make a call, you need to be paying attention rather than playing with your phone. Text messages are also great when you are at a loud club with friends. Text messages are perfect for sending someone information they will need later, such as, "When you get to the gate, punch in 27642 as the access code." Other than that, if you can send a text message, then you have your phone, so just use the phone. Do not use code in your text messages such as "LOL! SO R U L8 2?" because it's even more impersonal, and there is no guarantee the other person understands. Never send more than one text message at a time (160 characters) unless you are giving people directions... call them!

If you are flirting via text message, do not expect or need a reply. Flirting via text message is a "throw and forget" proposition. If you want to bond with a girl, CALL HER! Also, keep in mind that not 100% of text messages get through. Cell phone text/sms networks are not perfect. Voicemail always gets through. I will say though that I do enjoy occasionally taking a picture on my cell phone of something interesting and sending it to girls. Just be careful with this one. It's about your intent. If you send the picture with the intent of saying, "Hey, look, I am cool," it will backfire. If it's more like "Isn't this amusing?" you will be golden.

In business, email is great to make announcements, work on back-burner projects, and most important, track what has been said and agreed to. Email is great for when you cannot talk on the phone. It is great when talking on the phone is inconvenient. Email can be used whenever you have a logical reason to use it, but you want to use the phone as much as possible. Keep your email messages short and to the point. Email is a tool of efficiency, and the cost of that is that it is impersonal. Also, keep in mind that not 100% of email messages get through. Spam filters make email delivery imperfect. Voicemail always gets through.

Socially, email is completely worthless. The point of being social is interaction with people. It's like the Internet chat rooms that get used by social rejects! GET OUT OF YOUR HOUSE AND BE SOCIAL IN REAL LIFE! The only reason for social email is planning live get-togethers. The only other thing it's good for is sending jokes, and in my opinion that is just

a big waste of time. Use that time to GET OUT OF
YOUR HOUSE AND BE SOCIAL IN REAL LIFE!

Do not participate in Internet romance. Online
dating is not dating! This is an oxymoron. You can
shop for a car online, read a book online, and do
banking online, but you cannot "date" online anymore
than you can get a girl pregnant online. Call it what it
is: "finding girls online that you may actually date," at
which point, either date her for real or stop talking with
her. Yes, you can use the Internet as an additional
means to meet girls, but your goal is to get talking on
the phone as quickly as possible. Then you use the
phone to meet in person as quickly as possible. Got it?
It's all about live interaction.

I do not do Internet dating anymore. It is just so
much easier to walk up to girls I see in real life and get
to know them. If you are into Internet dating because
you are afraid to talk to strangers in real life, stop now
and get over it. Start talking to people. If you are
approaching girls in real life and also using Internet
dating as a supplemental tool, so be it (even if I still
think all Internet dating is stupid because it's non-social
dating; the concept is just flawed). For those people,
the following was how I escalated when I was still
doing it. After two emails I would say something like,
"Hey, let's talk on the phone like normal people,"
implying that if she did not go along with the idea, she
was being weird. The second time I talked with her on

the phone, I would say something like, "Hey, let's meet at the mall for lunch on…" and if she was not up for meeting in a public place in the middle of the day, I would accuse her of being 700 pounds, and tell her I'm just not much of a talk-on-the-phone guy. Get the interaction to the live stage as fast as possible and if she isn't into it, forget about her. If this method doesn't work well for you, stop Internet dating and approach strangers the way normal men do.

Everything you have just read will naturally evolve into your personality as you become more social, with more friends, more options, and better relationships. All of it comes from an ever-growing sense of self-value. Most people have to figure all this out on their own. You have the advantage of knowing the guidelines of the game as you learn to play it.

Next we are going to look at specific differences between the male and female brain and how these differences affect communication. Once you understand the differences, I will show you how to capitalize on your new understanding.

Science Not Sexism

Everyone knows that there are physical differences between men and women. These physical differences affect functionality. A man cannot get pregnant or give birth to a baby. Men have more testosterone and tend to be stronger. There are also differences between the male and female brain that explain the differences between male and female communication.

Most of you know that the brain is physically divided into two sides called hemispheres. The two hemispheres are not the same and serve different purposes. The left hemisphere is responsible for things like logic and memory. The right hemisphere is responsible for feelings, creativity, and imagination. These facts apply to a male brain as much as a female brain. The difference is in the connective tissue between the two hemispheres that allow them to talk to each other. Women have, on average, 30% more connective tissue. The medical names for these parts are the *corpus callosum* and the *anterior commissure*.

IT IS SCIENTIFIC FACT THAT THE MALE AND FEMALE BRAIN ARE PHYSICALLY DIFFERENT, AND THIS DIFFERENCE AFFECTS HOW THEY FUNCTION!

Now, I can hear some of you saying, "But it is just a small part of the brain and it's only 30% bigger, so how much effect could that have?" Let me put it this way. If I push a three-inch nail into your brain, how much total volume of your brain does it disturb? Less than 0.22% (the size/displacement of the modern human adult brain is about 1350 cc, and the size/displacement of a three-inch nail is less than 3 cc). And what is the most likely result of changing this less than 0.22% of your brain? Very, very, bad things. I think you are beginning to see the point here. When it comes to the human brain, a very small change alters everything.

Because of this connective tissue, women use more of their brain for every thought compared to men who use less of their brain for every thought. Women tend to use both hemispheres at the same time, and men tend to use one side at a time. In men, the communication system is not there to fully facilitate both sides working on the same thing at the same time. There you have it, women. Drawk Kwast just said, "Men use less of their brain at any given time."

But wait! Using more of your brain is not necessarily a good thing. It is true that this enables women to have an almost magical intuition, on average about 10 times better than an average guy. But here is the problem. Sometimes, simpler is better. Simpler is faster. It takes longer for two hemispheres to create an answer than one because they need to converse with each other during the process. The bigger problem arises when they do not agree and waste time arguing. The two hemispheres fighting is the classic example of a "woman not being able to make up her mind." For a woman, both logic and emotion participate and compete every time something goes through her brain. A man tends to use either logic or emotion. This is one of the reasons, besides testosterone, that men are better at sports. A right-handed man throwing a baseball tends to use only his left hemisphere (the right hand is controlled by the left hemisphere because the brain and body are cross-wired). A right-handed woman throwing a baseball engages her right hemisphere as well as the left hemisphere and overcomplicates the process with unnecessary thinking.

> *A good analogy would be if you were driving a car and you kept on asking your passenger advice before you took any action. Sooner or later you would crash the car from overcomplicating things and slowing your reaction time down too much. It would sound like, "Oh no, truck pulling out in front of me. What should I do? Should I..." [crashing sound!] It's just too slow.*

Men who are hearing this for the first time are thinking, "OK, that sounds logical." Some of the women are saying, "Well, that sounds logical, but I don't *feel* like it's true." Yes, exactly my point! You cannot argue with science. When scientists do active brain scans of men and women as they think, process information, and do the same tasks, what do they see? They actually see the active areas of the brain light up, and they get a graphical representation of what I just told you.

So how is this relevant? When you're talking with a woman, you need to feed both sides of her brain at the same time. The fewer senses you have to work with, the more difficult this becomes yet the more important it is to do. The following example illustrates how most guys screw this up.

> *Stephen meets Brenda at a nightclub. They make out on the dance floor, and she gives him her phone number. Stephen calls her a few days later and invites her to his place to cook dinner together. Stephen's thinking is simple. She already made out with him, gave him her phone number, and answered his call. The next logical step is that she comes over to his place and has sex with him. It's a sure thing, right? Stephen, like most guys, is ignoring the other half of the equation, the other half of her brain. No matter how "logical" that next step is, if he doesn't spend some time on that call feeding her emotional side and making her **feel** good about continuing in that direction with him,*

he's going to spend next Saturday night alone wondering what went wrong.

Whether its business or pleasure, if you ignore the feeding of her emotional side, you will only become frustrated as your logic continues to fail. Focus more on making her feel good about an idea and less on getting her to think an idea is good. If she isn't following your lead on something, change her mood, not her mind. This is powerful enough to work even if she is upset. Realize that you will never be able to get a logical point across when she is upset. Never, ever argue logic with an upset woman. You will **NEVER** win. When she is upset, you need to deal with her feelings first. After her mood is neutral, you can start using logic in tandem again. If you can get her in a good enough mood, logic will again take a backseat for her, but this time it will be in your favor. All you have to remember is that if she is very upset, logic tends to turn off, and she will go against you. If she is very happy, logic tends to turn off, and she will go with you. If her mood is somewhere in the middle, logic is part of the equation. The biggest advantage you have in any situation is to get her in a good mood and keep her there.

Women and the Power of Acknowledgment

The biggest complaint that women have is that guys do not listen. The biggest complaint men have is that women talk so much without making a point. This all goes back to how our brains are different, and can be extremely annoying to guys until they understand one thing that turns all of this into a very powerful tool. That one thing is the magical power of acknowledgment. To put this in more accurate terms, which you can now understand, this is feeding the emotional side of her brain the *feeling* of acknowledgment.

Have you ever tried to give a woman advice and she just gets upset? She didn't want a solution. She just wanted to talk about it. Here is the magic. Talking about it, even without a solution, is the solution. Sometimes all you need to do is listen to her, tell her that your hear her, and tell her that you understand how she *feels*. That's it. Just feed the emotional side of her brain. You do not necessarily have to give advice, fix anything, or even agree with what she is saying. You just need to listen. This is the number one reason why women use the phone: to get that feeling.

When it's business, I limit my "feeling acknowledgment sessions" with women to no more than five to ten minutes. I will usually start by saying something like, "I want to spend three minutes listening to you so I can understand how you *feel* about this." It's then very important to actually pay attention to what she says, or she will get very upset that you are simply placating her. She knows the difference. If you are listening, you are asking questions. If you are placating her, all she hears is a lot of "ah," "OK," and "sure." Once it's over, I usually forget everything she said about seven seconds later, but from time to time she actually brings up a good point that I had not considered.

Use this power of acknowledgment outside of business and be prepared to make an evening out of it. Don't be surprised if she tells you in the middle of the conversation that she's on the way to your house. When you're new to this game, sitting though it can drive you a little nutty, but keep in mind that the longer you sit there doing almost nothing, the more she gets the feelings she needs and the more likely you're about to get laid.

How to Get a Cute Girl's Phone Number

One of the big questions guys want answered is how to get a phone number from a girl they just met. It is true, as rumored, that I know a bunch of tactics for that, but I am going to be really honest with you here and tell you that you do not need training wheels. It's not what you say; it's how you say it. Do it with confidence and the words become irrelevant. The other problem that fancy training-wheel tactics create is a belief in your head that you do not have enough value to just ask for a girl's phone number. If you believe that you need to trick her into giving you her number, you've got bigger problems. You don't need to trick her. Just show enough value to make her want to give you her phone number. Remember, it's all about value.

Her name was Lena. At that point in my life, she was the cutest girl I had ever laid my eyes on. I was in Newport Beach having dinner at the Cheesecake Factory with some business associates when I suddenly found myself very distracted. There was no thinking involved. I looked at her, she caught me admiring her, and a second later, I found myself on my feet walking toward her table with no idea what I was going to do or say. I left the people at my table very confused at why I stopped talking to them midsentence and wondering where I was going. She was having dinner with her mom, brother, and brother's girlfriend. She smiled as I came closer. Without a plan, what came out of my mouth was, "Hello. You are adorable. Would you like to make a new friend over coffee some time?" She said yes. Everything in my body went tingly! That was when I realized that I did not have a pen or paper to get her phone number with. For some reason, instead of asking if anyone at the table had a pen, I told her that I would be right back and that I was going to go get a pen from the hostess booth. As I walked away, I overheard her mom telling her to just get my number because it would be "safer that way." When I got back to the table, I asked her for her phone number. She responded with, "Ah, just give me yours, and I can call you." I pulled back and told her, "That's OK. If you were as interested in seeing me again as I am in seeing you again, you would feel comfortable giving me your number." She grabbed the pen and scrap of paper out of my hand and wrote her number down. I cannot remember anything about that business dinner other than what I just told you. I do remember leaving the restaurant wondering how I managed to pull that off. Up until that night, I did not think that what I had just done was even possible. About a year after that, "not possible" had become "frequently repeatable." I was a new man, and I had a very big smile on my face.

Never apologize for being attracted to someone. Never be afraid to walk away. Be in the moment when doing is more important than thinking. The thrill is in the action, not the thought.

As I practiced more, on rare occasions when I asked for a girl's number, she would offer me an email address. I would never accept it. My rule is to take a phone number or walk away, no exceptions. If she told me she didn't have a phone, I would tell her that's a shame and just smile at her. If she told me she had a bad experience once when she gave her phone number out, I would tell her that being called by me would be a great experience and then just smile at her as if I knew I was going to get the number. If I didn't get it, I walked away. As it is now, 97 out of 100 girls whose phone number I ask for will give it to me, and I always get real numbers. And yes, anyone can learn to get these results. It just takes practice.

So how do I get phone numbers from girls now? The method I use 95% of the time is surprisingly easy. Once I know I have value with them, I simply say, "Give me your phone." Now mind you, at this point in the conversation, "give me your wallet" may even work. Remember, V-A-L-U-E! Sometimes they will ask why (as they are handing me their phone), and I will explain what I am doing as I am doing it. I say, "I am going to put my number in your phone and hit send so we have each other's numbers." Once my phone starts ringing, I hit "end call" on their phone, then "save to contacts" and save my name with my number in their phone.

That's it. Very simple. Never a fake number, lost piece of paper, or girl who is too nervous (or intoxicated) and types her number in wrong. Most of the time, shortly after that, I will use the camera on my phone to take a picture of us together. Later, I will use the picture to make a head shot of her to put in my contacts. This is very cool when you meet lots of people. From that point forward, every call, email, and text message I get from her has her picture on it. When she calls, I see her picture on my phone, which is very handy when you have a hard time remembering her name. Most of the time, I will later type notes into my contacts on where and when we met, and anything else I want to remember about her. I use the notes section of my contacts database for everyone I add, business or pleasure.

Calling Attractive Women

It's not a big deal. There is nothing magical about the phone. I remember when I got good at cold-approach pickup. I thought getting a girl's phone number was about three inches from the finish line. In my time I have collected thousands of phone numbers, but I have not slept with thousands of women, yet. So just relax and chill out. You are just getting started. All you are doing is continuing the adventure that started when she met you. Keep your cool, because if you sound like it's a big deal, you are going to lose. Women can hear the "you're the only girl I have talked to on the phone in years" desperation in your voice, and they will run from it.

Attraction first. Be sure that you have built up enough value with women before you ask for their phone number. It's just like sex. Girls need foreplay, and guys are ready instantly. Spend some time building their desire first. This is the only way to be sure that they actually want to talk to you again. You need to learn where this point is, because it's much further out than you think. The only way to figure this out is to build attraction with girls and then slowly walk away from them. Sooner or later you will have one grab you as you slowly start to walk off and ask for your phone number. After that happens a few times, you will notice that the quiet ones will not chase you, but they will give you the "doggie dinner bowl look" as you say goodbye. (This is the glazed-over look a puppy will give you as you put food in its bowl.) Once you become aware of how to gauge this, you will be able to speed the process up with practice. Most importantly, once you open your awareness to it, forget about it. You never want to become reactionary with women. You will kill your game by constantly wondering if you should be going for the phone number. Women can smell that lack of confidence, and it will kill everything. Always go for the phone number but never in a needy way, and play the timing as best you can. This is one of the Zen-like paradoxes that I spend quite a bit of time on during one-on-one training. The phrase I use is "awareness without diversion of intent."

Have valid reasons. This alone makes everything easier. It takes a little more time and effort but is well worth it. As a bonus, it can help solve the "I don't know what to talk about when I meet girls" problem. It also solves the "I don't know what to say when I call her" problem. I know this information is going to blow the minds of most men reading this, but it helps greatly to get to know a little about a girl before you ask for her phone number. Sure, any rule can be broken. I have successfully walked up to a girl and said, "You are adorable, and I am already running late. Give me your phone number and I will call you to discuss the absurd randomness of life sometime." Anyway, here is why you want to talk with her more. **Have a reason for liking her.** The girl needs to qualify herself to you. She needs to believe that you like her for more than just her looks. She needs to tell you a little about herself before you can do that. If you don't know anything about her, you are just another guy who wants to fuck her. Instead, you want to get excited when she tells you that she has traveled the world, etc. **Have a reason for calling her.** Randomly saying, "Hey, what's your number?" as you leave basically says, "Hey, I'm just some guy who wants to try to fuck you later." When you talk with her and find out she loves Thai food, it becomes very easy later in the conversation to simply say, "Hey, let's go for Thai food sometime...What's your phone number?" **Have a reason for continuing the conversation past getting the phone number.** Most guys get the phone number and run off. This says, "Now that I have your phone number, I can call you later and try to fuck you." Do not make the phone number into the goal of the interaction. The goal of the interaction is that you both enjoy the interaction. After you have the phone number, hang in there a while and finish the conversation.

How long to wait. This is one of the stupidest and most debated topics among men regarding dating. The only reason you would purposely wait is if her attraction to you is weak, and you need to use the "why hasn't he called me yet?" method of upping your value. Look, when it's on, it's on. Strike when the iron is hot (just make sure you do not come off as needy or as if you have nothing going on in your life). Focus on building attraction when you meet her, and the rest takes care of itself. Most of the time I will send a little text message that same night reminding her of something funny or unique that happened when we met. It will be something like, "I still cannot believe the pink sweater that guy was wearing." (Keep it simple. Keep it short.) About half of the time, my first call is the next day, and I may not ask her out until my next call a few days later. Don't overthink this.

Number of calls. No more than once a day. No more than three and no less than two in the first week. After that, if you still haven't gotten her on the phone, consider calling once every two weeks or so until you literally forget about her because you're too busy collecting other numbers. After the first week without getting her on the phone, you should only be using the number as a "warm-up" number anyway (to be defined later). Once you get her on the phone, relax and set up a time to see her again on that call or the next one. After that, you should be seeing her no more than once a week and talking once or twice a week for no more than 25 minutes each time. The closer she is to you, the less time you spend on the phone. The further away she is, you will need to spend a little more time on the phone (45 minutes max per call) to build strong enough feelings of desire that she will jump on a plane to see you (and remember, she has to cover at least some of the cost of coming to see you, even if it's just the cost of her luggage). Maintain plenty of space for at least the first two months to give her the gift of missing you.

Leaving voicemail. Below is the exact script I used for years. Please keep in mind that you are not the only person reading this, so I recommend changing it up a bit to fit your personal style. I can just see some poor girl saying to herself, "That's odd. That's the exact same message that Randy guy left me last week."

First Call: *"Hello <nickname I gave her that she will remember>. The weirdest thing just happened to me. Call me back at (321) 555-1212." I would not use my name because I was sure she would remember the nickname I gave her. NOTE: I already had a fun/cute/amusing story to tell when she called back.*

Subsequent Calls (if need be): *"Hey, its Drawk," followed by a short (about 40 seconds) odd, fun, amusing, story. NOTE: after the first call, I never left my phone number (she has Caller ID anyway) or ever ask her to call me back. I was being interesting to bait a call back, not asking for a call back. This was especially helpful if she was intent on not calling back, because I would get*

more calls in while being less needy, and
sometimes I'd be entertaining enough to change
her mind. Once she returned a call, if I got
voicemail again, I spoke in statements, never
questions.

If someone else answers. This is one of my personal favorites. If another girl answers her phone and asks to take a message, I ignore it, ask her who she is, and start to charm her for a short time. (I am sure to mention my name as part of the charming.) Then I get off the phone without leaving a message. If she asks to take a message as I am ending the call, I just say, "Oh, no message. Ta-ta for now." Properly charming the girl who answered the other girl's phone is much more powerful than any message I could have left.

Spend some time talking. Do not call just to make the date and then get off the phone. This is what you do with guys: conquer the phone call. As we all know, women like to talk on the phone for the chance to talk, so spend a few minutes reminding her of your personality (why she likes you) before you ask her out. Take her on a "small emotional ride of distraction," and when you know you have taken her mood up a notch, then you can make plans. Sometimes I'll call the first time without asking her out. I call just to raise her mood and remind her of my personality. I'll call a few days later and ask her out. Sometimes she will call me first. And remember, if there is the slightest hint of her needing to end the call, you must do so first. Be sure she is enjoying the call.

Comfort. Time on the phone with women counts as time they feel they are getting to know you. You do not need to make a date every time you call. They enjoy just talking to you from time to time. Be a part of their life.

Not calling from home. I do not recommend calling new numbers from home. I make my first calls while I'm out at a public place with "people-having-fun noise" in the background. What better way to suggest that I'm always having fun? Keep in mind that I really am having fun, not just going out to make the call. The best times to call are Tuesday, Wednesday, and Thursday early evenings from the patio of a bar. Girls always ask where I am. I usually answer that I am out at a bar that my friends invited me to, and I have about five minutes before they arrive. If you make habit of this method, don't be surprised when one of the girls eventually asks if she can join you.

Women and the word *no*. For some odd reason, women do not like to use the word *no*. Maybe it has something to do with their maternal instinct. Maybe they would just rather not hurt your feelings. For whatever reason, "no" just doesn't come out of their mouths when that is what they mean. So here is what you need to do as a guy to navigate this strangeness. First, when you ask a girl out, be direct and specific. Never call a girl and say, "Do you want to go out sometime?" This is very weak because the answer you will get 95% of the time will be "sure, sometime," and in reality, you just got nothing. You want to say, "I am going to Zen Bar for sushi this Thursday at 5:30. Would you like to join me?" Beyond the fact that this is a much more decisive and confident statement, it will keep things easy when you are decoding her response. There are only three responses you can get when you are specific like this. The first is, "Yes." OK, it's on! The second is the counteroffer. This one is simple to figure out. She says, "I don't like sushi. Can I talk you into a steak house?" She might say, "I need a little more time to get ready. How about 6:30?" or "I work late that night. How about Friday?" The point is that she gives you a second option when what you suggested will not work. She is being creative to help make it happen. She is suggesting options to make it work. And the last option is anything else that comes out of her mouth, and you can simply hear it as "no." If you ask her out for sushi, 5:30, Thursday, and she tells you she has to wash her cat, that is a "no" because she did not give a counteroffer. She is just trying to let you down easy. Move on. Never, ever, under any circumstances, give her a counteroffer to your original offer; it's very weak. She is allowed to make the counteroffer. You are not. GET IT THROUGH YOUR HEAD that there are only three possible options: (1) yes, (2) her counteroffer, or (3) no. There is never a fourth option, ever. And when she doesn't say yes or give you a counteroffer, don't make a big deal out of it.

Setting up the first date. First things first. Never use the word *date* with a woman. You are hanging out, having dinner, playing pool, or saving whales. Call it by the activity you are actually doing together. If she calls it a date while you are together, give her a sly smile and say, "I thought we were just having dinner," while you pull her in for a little hug. Girls do this to us all of the time. It's called sending mixed signals. I enjoy using their own methods against them to build attraction. Anyway, if you followed my advice on how to set up getting the number and everything went as planned, your "date" is already set up. I am talking about the example above, when you used the reason for getting Thai food together sometime to get her phone number. Every guy I know does this backwards. You must first get her excited about doing something with you and **then** go for the number. You have a far better chance of getting the number that way, and you will not be wondering what to do later. If you somehow got a phone number without seeding a date, you will need to know the following: the easiest way to get her out is to ask her to join you on something you are already doing.

This is a great way to do it if she ends up turning you down because you were clearly not going out of your way to plan anything special; she was just invited to join in on what you were already planning to do. You are doing it either way. This could be going wine tasting with friends or out to a ball game with a group of people. Don't worry so much about the group event. If it goes well, you can always isolate and pounce on your prey later in the evening. One of my favorites is telling a girl that I suffer from being terminally straight and I need new clothes. I ask if she will join me shopping and play dress-up with her new life-size Ken doll. I told one girl while I was in California to come over and I'd take her shopping. She was so confused when we pulled into the grocery store parking lot. I explained that I never know what brand of toilet paper to buy. She got a good laugh out of it, and we made dinner together that night.

Practice

There is nothing worse than sitting around in your empty apartment for hours contemplating your first call to a gorgeous woman who liked you enough to give you her phone number. This is what I refer to as the long, drawn-out process of failure. The longer you sit there thinking about it, the worse the call will go. The odd thing is that if you just picked up the phone and called her without overthinking, you would get much better results. The best state to call girls in, however, is when you have already been talking to girls. Stop thinking and just start calling while saving the important calls for after you are warmed up. Here is how you do it.

Keep your old dead phone numbers and use them as warm-up numbers. I have "warm-up" as a category in my phone that I can sort my numbers by (with about a dozen other categories). You should be getting numbers from everyone, even girls you do not want to sleep with, because you need warm-up numbers. Collect as many numbers as you can. Just do not do it in a needy way. Yet another paradox: the easiest time to get numbers is when you already have too many of them. Anyway, you need to make a few calls until you are comfortable and in a talkative mood before you call one you actually care about. If you get voicemail, fine. Be creative and have fun with it. If she answers and it doesn't go well, laugh. Who cares? Not you. You may even have something positive happen from a warm-up. I like to call girls who I have totally ruined and do it like nothing happened. If they get rude, I use the line, "You are underestimating my ability to hang up on you right now." It's fun, and the real calls always seem to go so much better.

What do you talk about on the warm-up calls? Anything you want. It doesn't matter, remember? You do not care about these numbers, and that is why you are using them for warm-up. Call a girl and tell her you are thinking of switching from boxers to briefs and ask her opinion. Then ask her why she "feels" that way. Tell her you want her opinion about changing your hairstyle. Your barber is recommending it, but he's gay and you think he has a crush on you. Tell her that the valet got diarrhea in your car while returning it to you last night, and you're wondering if you should sue. Just have fun with it. Keep her entertained and engaged in the conversation with short stories followed by questions, and keep her on the phone as long as you can. The trick is that once you have gone through a few warm-up numbers, go immediately to your real call without thinking about it.

If you don't have any warm-up numbers yet, call random numbers until you get a girl, and come up with creative ways to keep her on the phone as long as you can. Here are a few samples from some of my more humorous warm-up calls.

Girl 1:   Hello.

Me: Hello is Becky there?

Girl 1:   No, I think you have the wrong number.

Me: Oh no, not again...Well, will you be my friend?

Girl 1:   Ah, I'm not sure if that would be a good idea.

Me: Why? You seem nice. I bet you send your friends Christmas cards every year.

Girl 1:   Are you serious?

Me: No, I'm Drawk. What is your name?

Girl 1:   Oh, you're drunk. Ahhhh...

Me: No, I am Drawk, D-R-A-W-K. That's my name. You're not going to spell it wrong on my Christmas card, are you!?!

Girl 1:   [click, followed by dial tone]

Girl 2: Hi.

Me: Hello, is Martha there?

Girl 2: You have the wrong number.

Me: You sound a lot like my dead grandmother.

Girl 2: [All I could hear was breathing.]

Me: I still have the scarf you knit me when I was five years old.

Girl 2: [click]

That one didn't go so well, but I just about pissed myself, I was laughing so hard.

Girl 3: [Voicemail picks up.] Hi, this is Susan. Leave a message. [Beep]

Me: Hi. Susan. Ah, this is awkward. Um, I think I know you, but I am not sure of that or even my name right now. I just woke up in the hospital with amnesia. I have been unconscious for a little over a week. They found me on the beach with no wallet or ID, but I had your number on a scrap of paper in my left pocket. I am hoping you know me and can help me answer some questions. I am six-foot-one, about 230 pounds, muscular build, dark hair, with a beard. I am white, and they guess I'm about 27 to 32 years old. They gave me a disposable cell phone, so you can call me back at (321) 555-1212. [Yes, I gave my real number.] And if you are my girlfriend, I'm OK baby.

Me: [She called back.] Hello.

Girl 3: Um, hi. I don't think I know you, but it wouldn't be the first time something happened that I don't remember while out drinking.

Me: They did say I had alcohol in my system when they found me. What day was that?

Girl 3: The Friday before last.

Me: Well, that makes sense, I mean as far as this being possible, at least.

Girl 3: Yeah, this is so weird. Are you OK?

Me: Yeah, I'm OK, just really confused.

Girl 3: I guess that makes two of us.

Me: The doctors said it might kick-start my memory if I were to get around familiar places and people. Would you be willing to meet me at the beach for lunch?

Girl 3:   Um, OK. Where? [Silly girl. California girls can be amazingly dumb.]

Me: How about... [And she was as cute in person as she was dumb on the phone.]

Girl 4:   Hello.

Me: Oh, I think I have the wrong number. Ah, you probably know this though as well as Veronica. I'm on the way to the Mission Mall for a lunch, but I have never been there before. What's a good restaurant?

Girl 4:   I like the New York Sam's.

Me: Thanks! Want to join me?

Girl 4:   Ah... [click]

Me: I guess not.

Warm-up calling random phone numbers is like crank-calling for adults. It's fun. Just don't do anything illegal, and don't hurt people.

In my time "practicing phone skills," I have had sex with girls I had written off months before, and one time I met a girl for lunch whose number I called by mistake. My claim to fame (after years of practice) was a cold call from someone trying to sell me some kind of credit repair service. After 45 minutes on the phone with her, I had seen a picture on MySpace and talked her into visiting me in Las Vegas. Welcome to my world. **Sometimes being lucky enough to succeed involves being stupid enough to try.** Anything is possible. As far as business, do as instructed above, and as you practice in the social arena, you will see results that spill into business.

Remembering Your Goals

One of the things completely amazing to me is that guys will get so involved in learning these tools that they forget the goals of using them. Business is simple. You collect contact info after you have made an impression (so they remember you and what your function is) on people you see as having value. This is done very easily with the exchange of business cards. Your goal is to have them call you if they see an opportunity or to have them return your call if you see an opportunity. Don't overcomplicate it.

With women, it's all about being out and enjoying your time with them. What I cannot understand is why a guy would walk up to a girl at a bar, spend a few minutes talking with her, and ask for her phone number so "they can go out sometime." This is completely idiotic! He was already "out with her." Why the hell would he walk off, only to attempt orchestrating a duplicate of the situation he was already in? So the next time you meet a cute girl while picking up your dry cleaning, don't ask for her phone number after getting her to giggle like a schoolgirl. Invite her to join you for lunch right now at the café next door. Remember, you can't have sex with a phone number.

Power Communication Part 7
Humor

Week 7

There is something ironic about writing a technical document on humor because humor, or rather the idea of what is funny and is not funny, is so variable depending on the audience, their mood, the environment, what they've had for breakfast, and about nine million other possible factors. Humor is one of those uniquely human and complex concepts that is difficult to explain in a logical way. Have you ever noticed that a joke ceases to be funny when you have to explain it? The purpose of this part of the book is to explain the concept of humor as it affects the social equation. Laughter is a social response. Understanding the underlying mechanisms that produce laughter will increase your social power.

I wish I could have found a way to make this section of the book shorter. It would have been quicker if I could have simply given you the answer to what humor is on these first few pages, but unfortunately, I can't teach you about the destination without first taking you on the journey. Stick with me for the journey and you'll receive the reward. To truly understand humor from all its angles is to gain a unique new power. Let's get started...

All She Wants Is a Guy Who Can Make Her Laugh?

When I was in high school, there were many things that did not make any sense to me. One of these things was the answer I got from girls when I asked what the number one thing was that they wanted in a guy. Every time, the answer was a guy who could make them laugh. I was confused by this answer because I was good at getting girls to laugh, but the giggles never resulted in actually getting the girl. I remember at one point concluding that I had the cause-and-effect relationship backwards. I thought that if you go too long without sex, you lose your sense of humor, and if you get laid enough, you stay in a good mood and keep your sense of humor. I was sure that sooner or later I would lose my virginity or my ability to make girls laugh. By the time I made it to college (this was age 16 for me), I hadn't lost either.

In college I started from scratch. As I looked for a new cause-and-effect relationship, it appeared that being athletic, popular, and having enough money for an incredibly fast car was what got the girls. So I made a few changes happen in my life very quickly. I was running a computer consulting company at the time and put all my efforts into that, or rather all my efforts into making money. I knew that with enough money, I could get both the car and popularity. It worked. At age 18, I was driving a car around the college campus that no one could believe was mine. It turned the heads of girls, guys, faculty, everyone. Getting that car changed my reputation literally overnight.

The birth of a good rumor happens when fiction makes more sense than reality, and this was how my new reputation was born. The rumor was that I had become a drug dealer and that the computer thing was just a cover for that. I guess it was easier to believe that the money came from selling drugs rather than computers. I was now notorious and one of the most talked-about people on campus. This gave me the social ability to "sit at any table I wanted to at lunch." I frequented both the "cool table" and the "jock table." I wanted the girls who sat at the cool table, and I wanted help from the guys at the jock table to get in better shape to get those girls. I remember the day I realized that my plan was working and that it was now time to get the girl, and this girl's name was Amy.

I had noticed her many months before. She was perfect, so full of energy, and I remember how nervous I was the first time I talked with her. Months before, I couldn't even look her in the eyes because it just felt as if she were so much above what I could ever hope to be with. The car, money, and popularity changed this self-value problem. Looking back now, I realize however that I could have done it without the car, money, and popularity, if I could have just believed I was good enough for her without it, but a concept like this would never have made sense to me back then. In either case, it didn't matter. I had the car, money, and popularity, and most importantly, I had a date with Amy next Thursday. Life was good.

To this day, I still look back on that Thursday with a huge smile on my face. In that moment, that perfect moment, I had everything that mattered to me. I had a great feeling of accomplishment as my dream girl sat in my dream car next to me.

It wasn't long after that night that I realized something. Amy didn't make me laugh. Sure, she was a great girl with huge boobs, and I loved the way she smelled, but something was missing. Somehow we never "clicked," so to speak. Maybe the girl I had made her out to be in my head was totally different from who she actually was. I think that's the danger of actually getting your dream girl out on a date. After lusting for her from afar, you find out she is different from the person you dreamed her to be. If she had made me laugh, would we have clicked? I remember the realization that I needed more than a great girl with huge boobs. I needed to be able to laugh with her. This realization confused the hell out of me. It's a very strange thing to get everything you want, only to figure out something's missing. Why would I care if she could make me laugh? Maybe there was something to this laughter thing after all, but what was it?

One day, I am having lunch at the cool table when the next two realizations hit me. Sure, I am at the cool table, but I am still me. I am the same person I was before the popularity, car, and money. It is exactly as it was in high school. I am having lunch, and the people around me are laughing with me. The only difference is that in high school, it was the average kids laughing with me, and now I have the cool kids laughing with me. What is the difference? What changed? Why can I get the cool kids laughing now? What does this mean?

As more questions than answers hit me, my second realization surfaced. As I looked across the table in that moment at one of the most popular girls at school, I suddenly became aware of my intense attraction to her, mostly in my pants. She was one of those girls who is so hot that it doesn't even register. I think my ego had prevented a crush on her up until that point mostly because I knew I had no chance. Suddenly however, I realized that she was in fact now in my league. Her name was Ammie. Yes, same name, different girl, different spelling. At least I was being consistent.

Ammie, like any other uber-hot popular girl, had a boyfriend. I did not see this as a problem, however. I had a more expensive car and more money, and I was more popular than her current guy. I thought, by all logical calculations, this conquest should be easy. I just needed a plan. At that point in my life, I had learned one lesson correctly: **have a world that she wants to be part of, and she will be sucked into it.**

The money had afforded one additional thing by this point. I had a place in the hills, and the view was breathtaking. As I sat one night on my balcony watching the fireworks at Disneyland, I decided it was time to throw a party. My plan was very simple. Invite all the cool kids to a party at my place, everyone but her, and be sure everyone knew it was an open invitation for all. The chances of her showing up were very good if "everyone else is doing it." The party went great. I had a lot of fun. Everyone showed up but her.

Now I should probably mention here that the above plan was a sound one. For some odd reason, it didn't work the first time I thought of it. My guess is that she knew I was after her, and back in those days, I had yet to figure out the concept that girls need to be attracted to you BEFORE you jump all over them like a man on fire into a snowbank. Anyway, I started to use this tactic again years later with much more success.

The next time I was at the cool table, realization hit me yet again. Everyone at the table would laugh at my jokes. After the party, I was cooler with the guys, and some of the girls were paying much more attention to me. Coincidentally (or so I thought at the time), the girls who laughed most at my jokes were the ones I ended up dating later. Ammie, however, never laughed at my jokes. She always laughed at her boyfriend's jokes. It was odd because no matter how hard I tried, I couldn't get her to laugh, and it seemed like the harder I tried, the worse my results were. Her boyfriend, however, could do just about anything and she would laugh, even though he had less money, a dorky car, and fewer friends than I. This infuriated me to the point of inspiration as I created a new curse phrase… **FUCK DAMN IT!**

So, I thought to myself, "I have everything but cannot get this girl to laugh. Her boyfriend has nothing but he can make her laugh. The girl is with the guy who makes her laugh." But, I thought, if I had all the "stuff" she would choose me. What the hell? I have everything! Fuck damn it! Oh well. The car was fun and I was getting more girls than before… and coincidentally (or so I thought at the time) the girls I was getting all laughed at my jokes. But I knew I wouldn't have been able to get them without the "stuff." Or would I have? What if I would have just been able to figure out how to make them laugh?

I wouldn't figure these answers out for over a decade.

Always Laugh at the Boss's Jokes

So women confused the hell out of me, just like they confuse every other young man. I wasn't too bent out of shape about it though, because at least I was going out on more dates now. I might have not gained understanding, but my situation had at least improved. I think that this is one of the huge driving forces preventing people from reaching their full potential. People who are content with "better than before" rarely put energy into figuring out "better than that." So I focused my brainpower back on something I could make sense of: business.

One of the problems my new computer company had was high vendor pricing. I was able to get whatever product I needed, but I was paying too much for it. By the time I sold product to my customers, they were not getting that sweet a deal, and I wasn't making enough profit. I just didn't have the connections I needed to pull this off. I remember drinking out of a coffee mug as I was trying to figure out a solution to my challenge. The bottom of the mug had the words "Made in Korea" on it. This became the answer, as those three little words sparked an idea that changed my life.

I was in Koreatown. I knew I was in the right place when I couldn't see any English words anywhere. I was looking for local Koreatown magazines and newspapers with ads in them for computers. As I walked to the front of a Korean market, jackpot! I grabbed one of each and headed for home. It took some time, but I went through all of them and cut out every computer store advertisement. I then organized all of the ads from the same stores together. I was amazed at what I found. The price that these stores were selling at to any person off the street was lower than what I could buy at as a computer reseller from my vendors. It then occurred to me that even though Koreatown was only a few miles away, it was totally cut off from my world. You see, my business customers would never venture into Koreatown to buy computers, and the computer stores in Koreatown never ventured out of Koreatown to find clients in Newport Beach. My opportunity had been found in becoming an import/export business inside of California.

It wasn't easy. Finding a reputable vendor in Koreatown who spoke enough English and would do business with me was difficult. Most of the stores just sold me too many bad parts. Some I think even raised the prices just for me. Of the ones who provided decent parts at good prices, the relationship tended to fall apart over time because of cultural differences and communication issues.

As I walked through the door of the next Korean computer store, I noticed a man who looked like Mr. Miyagi with a bad comb-over. I was sure he was the one in charge because everyone else who worked in the store was focused on him and laughing at what seemed to be him telling some kind of story. I couldn't tell what he was saying because I don't speak Korean, but I do know that when the boss tells a joke, everyone laughs no matter what language he speaks. Anyway, he walked over to me when he noticed I had entered his store. Based on the look he gave me, I was sure that not too many white people came into his store. This seemed to be par for all the stores I had been to.

As he greeted me in a kind of "you're white, but I am willing to talk to you" way, I gave him a smile and took note that his English seemed not to be too bad. This made giving my pitch easier. After we talked for about 10 minutes, we decided to do some business together. If his product was good and my checks cleared, we might one day trust each other enough to make some real money. As I left the store, I realized that I had not asked him his name. His name sounded something like "Kioungsung." I smiled at him, put my hand on his shoulder, and told him that I was going to just call him Kenney. He laughed, and somehow in that moment I knew that we would be doing business together for years. What was it in that moment when he laughed that made me know this? Somehow that laughter broke some kind of tension. At that point, I knew he was cool with me. I would not fully understand this for years, but what I did understand was the importance of having my customers and vendors sharing a laugh with me. I thought it just put them in a good mood, but was there something more to it?

What Did This All Mean?

The day came years later when all the pieces finally came together. As with all truths, it was simple and right in front of me the whole time. I was just not able to see it until then. I was at a restaurant in Newport Beach. I was watching a man and woman on what appeared to be a date. I had guessed by their apparent discomfort with each other that it was a first date, possibly even a blind date. It was painful. The guy kept trying to joke with her, but she wasn't laughing. Worse than that, he was actually laughing at his own jokes, mostly because he was getting more uncomfortable by the moment. Then it happened. She laughed at something he said, and the energy between them completely changed in that instant. THAT WAS IT! Like Neo in *The Matrix* (1999), I had seen the underlying code. I didn't actually hear the laughter. Rather I could see the little green chunks of code between them, so to speak, and I could read what it was saying.

I immediately left the rich people of Newport Beach and headed for a burger joint in Buena Park to see if this was the same when people had less money. I witnessed the exact same thing, regardless of social status and wealth. My next stop was a coffeehouse, and it was all the same. I struck up a conversation with a girl there. When I made her laugh a little, I could see it there also as I created it, and I knew I would leave with her phone number. As I did, the theory had been tested. There is a certain calming pride that comes from realizations such as this. So what was it? What was I seeing in place of hearing laughter? The code was acceptance and approval. The equation is simple and universal: Laughter = Acceptance + Approval.

Women are not lying when they say that they really just want a guy who can make them laugh. Think about it for a second, and you'll realize that what they are actually saying is that they want a guy who they accept and approve of. The same holds true for men with women. Sure, one-night stands happen, but if I am going to be in a relationship, I need a girl I can laugh with. I need a girl I accept and approve of. So was the situation with Amy that I did not approve of her? Quite the opposite, actually. I felt as if I never deserved her. So why didn't I laugh with her? Simple: we do not laugh with people we are not comfortable with, and I was never comfortable around her because I thought she was too good for me. I couldn't accept the situation. My brain couldn't process the fact that I had won, so I never relaxed enough to enjoy it. And why do I still giggle to this day about getting my dream girl into my dream car for a date? Well, that one is about giving approval to myself for what was at the time my greatest feat.

As for my fitting in at the cool table, that one is simple. I was getting approval as they laughed at my jokes. It worked just as it had with the average kids in high school. I had just taken things up a notch because of my accomplishments. I felt that I fit in, and because of this, the cool kids agreed and showed it with their laughs of acceptance.

How about Ammie and her boyfriend? Well, I had more stuff than her boyfriend, but I could not make her laugh, so he won. If I could have gotten her laughing as much with me as she did with him, I would have won because of the stuff, but with no laughter, I lost, even with more stuff. Now you understand one of the reasons a pool boy can steal the heart of a millionaire's wife.

Last but certainly not least was my buddy Kenney. I gave him a nickname, and he responded with approval and amusement. Additionally, his laughter showed he was comfortable with me. This is how I did close to a million dollars of business with him over the years. He eventually gave me a $100,000.00 credit line and never even did a credit check. It's amazing how acceptance and a few years of trust can grow into something. I am sure he enjoyed the profits, as did I.

Just get yourself to see the approval and acceptance every time you hear someone laugh. Then all you have to do is see where the approval and acceptance is focused. For me, this habit is so ingrained into my communication perception that every time people laugh at something I have said, I see one of those cartoon bubbles above their heads saying something like "approval," "acceptance," "I like you," "sell it to me now," or "I want to have sex with you."

Laughing with Someone

What I have just explained above is known as "laughing with someone." The classic example is someone telling a joke and the person he told it to laughing back in approval/acceptance of him. Let's look at a stand-up comedian's act from this new perspective for a moment. I should probably mention at this point that in my quest to understand social interaction, I have ventured into the land of being an amateur comedian myself. If you think you have what it takes to make people laugh, try a few open mic nights at your local comedy club. When you can last four and a half minutes without leaving the stage crying, you have learned something.

Anyway, here is how this stuff works. Comedians are storytellers. Like any good storyteller, they suck their audience into their reality. One of the simplest formulas they can follow is to engage the senses of their audience, build a connection through commonality, and deliver a punch line. Here's an example:

> *I don't use the US Postal Service for anything. I use email, pay all my bills online, and know how to use a fax machine. I was bummed out the other day when my insurance company told me that I needed to mail them the original copy of something*

I had faxed them. This called for a field trip to my local post office. While I was there, I figured I would buy a page of stamps so that I had a few extra just in case I needed to mail the insurance company anything else. As I was deciding between Mickey Mouse Disney stamps and Bugs Bunny Looney Tunes stamps, I realized something. The stamp in the lower right of each page was not actually a stamp. The page had an odd number of stamps on it, and what should have been a stamp in the lower right corner of the page just said, "This block not valid postage." At first I was confused at why they didn't just print the page with a logical number of stamps and avoid this problem. Then I got a little insulted that the US Postal Service would think that I would miss the fact that one of the little stickers is missing the all-important cartoon animal making it legal and valid postage. I started to wonder if the guy in the back even notices what's stuck onto the envelope. Do they really check? So, I decided to mail a letter to myself with their "This block not valid postage" sticker where the stamp should go. Sure enough, a few days later, I got my letter. I think they should change the text on that sticker to read, "At the USPS, we're dumber than you."

Yes, this story actually happened. I tested it with every sticker I had, and it always worked. I hope I don't get arrested for mail fraud. If you caught yourself smiling a little, there are a few things that are most likely true for you. You probably don't think most of the people who work for the post office are very smart. You have probably had the post office screw something up before that caused you annoyance. You somehow feel that by my doing what I did, I got them back just a little for you and proved how dumb they can be. You approve of me messing with them. All of this is why you cracked a smile.

Laughing at Someone

Why do we laugh when someone trips over his own feet? Why do we laugh when someone stubs her toe? Why is it funny for someone to slip on a banana peel? All of these can be put together into the category of people doing something dumb and hurting or embarrassing themselves (but usually not in any permanent way; if it causes real permanent physical injury, we usually don't laugh unless it's a movie, and in that case, we know it's not real). None of this would be funny to anyone who has never done anything dumb and hurt or embarrassed himself before. I laugh at you when you stub your toe because I have stubbed my toe before. When I see you do it, I laugh out of a form of acceptance of you. I don't feel like the only idiot anymore. I know it hurts, I know you will be fine, and I don't feel so alone in my own personal stupidity. This is connection building humor. This is why movies such as *There's Something About Mary* (1998), *American Pie* (1999), and *The 40-Year-Old Virgin* (2005) are so funny. The next time people laugh at you doing something dumb, remember that they laugh only because they can relate.

There is one other type of laughing at someone. This is what the schoolyard bully does. This is the opposite of the connection-building humor I just described. This is mockery and is done to separate the person laughing from you. This is the classic example of people tearing others down to make themselves feel better. They label you as low value and disassociate from you, thereby suggesting that they don't have low value because they are not like you. (Anyone who remembers the explanation behind "don't think of a pink elephant" will find that very amusing.) This is the tactic of an empty person, and the empty life it will lead to will be the punishment. When someone uses this on you, be unaffected; you know that the person laughing at you has no real value. At the point that such people realize they have no effect on you, they will move on. The trick I use is that for whatever they say, all I can hear is "Wah wah wah wahhhh." I cannot have my feelings hurt because I do not understand them. I cannot fall into their frame because I cannot understand them. I will not argue with them because I do not know what they said. I look at them as if they are from Mars.

Playful Teasing

A little playful teasing now and again is healthy. It helps to remind us never to take anything too seriously. If you want to keep that childlike wonder that makes life worth living, you are going to have to remain playful. As adults, I think we need to relearn how to behave like children and get back what we lost in growing up. Sure, there is a time and place for everything but sadly, most adults have forgotten how to have fun. Of course, we all have responsibilities to fulfill, but I always fulfill them in the most enjoyable way I can.

I want to make serious money with people I don't need to be serious around all of the time. I am most interested in women who know how to have a serious relationship without being so serious. Most importantly, I enjoy being with people who know how to have serious fun.

Please do not mistake this for advice to screw around all the time. I am just saying to feel joy along with pride in whatever you are doing. Remember that I said humor is acceptance and approval. The point is that I want to be around people I accept and approve of and who accept and approve of me. I don't trust people who are serious 100% of the time. I guess you could say that I don't accept or approve of them.

You'll need to understand the difference between playfully teasing people and insulting them. To properly distinguish this, we first need to review the definition of communication. Communication is the message *as it is received.* The message you intended is irrelevant. So in reality, it doesn't matter what you say. What matters is how someone receives it. It's all about how the listener interprets your message, not what you actually said, that's important. So how do you know if you are teasing or insulting? If the listener is smiling, you are doing it right. If he or she is not, you did it wrong. Everyone is different, and it's always an ever-changing gray area.

Teasing is about 85% art and only 15% science. Like any art, it requires practice. Realize that you can easily tease your best friends. You are much more likely to insult a stranger by mistake than you are a longtime friend.

I WOULD LIKE TO REMIND YOU THAT EVERYTHING YOU ARE ABOUT TO READ IN THE FOLLOWING PAGES WAS DONE BY A PROFESSIONAL. DO NOT TRY ANY OF THE FOLLOWING YOURSELF WITHOUT DIRECT SUPERVISION BY A PROFESSIONAL, OR YOU MAY END UP BEATEN TO DEATH.

I am 100% pure-blooded German. I have a friend named Miles who is black. Now Miles is as black as I am white. Most "black" people are actually more brown than black. Miles is so black that I'd never play hide-and-seek with him at night. He would be cheating. I can make a joke like that about him because he and I have been friends for years. When he reads this, he will laugh, know I'm teasing him, and not feel insulted. Now if I were to meet him in a public place, such as a mall, and as I walked up to him I said, "What up, my nigga!?!" he would smile, as he shook his head a little. Any other black people around would look very closely at Miles' response to me. If he laughs, I'm fine, and all the other black people would know I'm cool. If, however, Miles' response suggested that I had insulted him, I would be in trouble with not just him but most likely every black person around. That is how this dynamic works.

Can I pull stuff like this off 100% of the time? Nope. But that is part of the thrill of learning how. I strongly recommend starting slowly, but I can tell you from personal experience that when it's gone wrong for me, the only major repercussion has been a great story to tell afterward.

While I was going through what I like to refer to as the pain period of learning how to cold-approach women, I fell on my face time and time again. It took thousands and thousands of approaches to learn what I know now, and most of those early approaches resulted in a horrific crash and burn. Sometimes it was so bad that the people who I was with pretended not to know me after I would get blown out. One of the funniest blowouts from saying the wrong thing happened in Irvine, California, at the Fox Sports Grill. I walked up to two gorgeous blondes who seemed like they could use a little injection of fun. One of the things you learn when you keep on going out is how bored most people are. I found it to be very easy to walk into a group that wasn't having much fun and make new friends. Anyway, I ran every bit of material I had to get their spirits up and put smiles on their faces, but they just kind of sat there as if they had been tranquilized. After about 40 minutes, I had nothing left. I just kind of stopped and looked at them. What came out of my mouth next was "OK, who died?" The shorter girl replied with "a good friend of ours last night." She was completely serious; of course I was completely shocked. Ah, the fun of cold-approaching. You never know what's going to happen. I ended up sticking in for about another 10 minutes and I actually walked away with the shorter one's phone number, although I'm not sure how I even pulled that one off. My guess is that she just figured that if she gave me her phone number, I would go away and leave them in peace. It turned out to be her real phone number, but I never did see her again.

With social interaction, you are never 100% sure of anything, so you may as well have some fun with it. Why risk insulting people? Well, as with gambling on the stock market, there can be a big payoff, and with practice you can get very good at getting that payoff. In the months to follow, I just got braver and braver. I wanted to find the limits and I was starting to see that they were a lot further out than I had ever thought. The following is copied directly from my personal journal:

Somehow it's always the last group of people in any given night that is the most interesting. Maybe it's because the longer I talk, the more my mojo flows, and the better I get. Maybe it's because the later it gets, the drunker the girls are. Maybe it's just that, as soon as I find some interesting people to talk to, I stay in, don't leave, and so they are the last group of people I will meet that night. This night definitely followed that rule. Interesting doesn't even come close to describing my last interaction of the night...

So it was Saturday night, and somehow Karl, Garrett, and Brian talked me into going out in Huntington Beach, California. I'm glad I did, even if I was still hung over from the night before. I guess nights like these are where my idea of "just do more" came from. Actually, on second thought, Karl got me started on that one.

It's a little after midnight, we were out on the patio, and the women we were talking with started to bore me. I left Karl as he was mesmerized by nipples. They were nice, but I was looking for an intellectual challenge inside of a hot beach body. I turned to my left to see two of Huntington Beach's finest, with attitude and then some: one a brunette and one a blonde. The blonde was showing the brunette a text message on her phone. I butted in with, "So what did he send you?" The dark haired one gives me a "spawn of Satan" look and says, "He said, GO AWAY!" It was probably the biggest "fuck you" I had ever got in response to an opener. I turned back to the group I had just left for a moment, which was still right behind me, before turning back to the two girls again.

As I turned back in, the brunette was giving the blonde advice on the guy who had sent her the text message. I interrupted to ask her if she was qualified to give advice; was she in a happy relationship? That's when things went nuclear!

What proceeded was about 25 minutes of some of the harshest "teasing" I have ever participated in. I was honestly just staying in for practice at that point, and thought it would end with either the blonde slapping me in the face or the brunette kicking me in the balls. The highlight was when the brunette sought validation from me by saying that she was in a 7-year relationship. I told her that doesn't count because he either left her because she wasn't good enough, or she left him because he was a dork. She answered with, "He was not a dork (note: so we know he left her), he is the father of my two children." I replied with, "How does you being willing to sleep with him twice not make him a dork?" At which point the blonde asks me if I just like fucking with people. I told her that I like ice-cream.

So anyway, I stay in. I do not get upset. I keep on treating them like unwanted red-headed stepchildren. Then the unexpected happens. They give up: I win. They just stop. The brunette looks at me, says she is cold, and wants to go inside. Now I'm thinking that she is talking to her friend, that they have had enough, and they are running away. To my amazement, she looks at me and says, "Aren't you coming with?" I'm asking myself at this point what planet I'm on. I just go with it, as if all the heated teasing never happened. I follow her in.

As soon as my friends figure out that I won them over, Garrett joins us, and then Karl. After about 5 minutes the brunette locks on Karl with the intent of figuring out how to get him in her mouth. I am with my target, the blonde, who cannot stop touching me for more than a few seconds at a time. At the point the brunette asked for my phone number, I knew it was time to move the girls to Brian's place, conveniently a two minute walk away.

On the walk back, the brunette established that Karl was just like all the other bad boys she dated, and is trying to avoid (translation, she will be calling me to get his phone number, after sleeping with him tonight; she will be stalking him in no time). It was a good night for Karl and me.

Sometimes you have to prove to people that you are at their level or better by teasing them a little. These girls were hot and accustomed to watching guys buy them drinks and then crumble under their bitchiness. Karl and I don't crack like that, which is why they went home with us. Oh, and I should probably mention that sometimes the girls don't smile about your teasing until they are in bed with you. How do you know if you did it right? You're having sex with them.

Now that you have read some examples, we need to dive into how it is that the harsher you are, the harder it is to get them to smile, and the better it works. Remember the base concept we are talking about here is approval/acceptance. With that in mind, the better you are at saying things that others could not get away with, the stronger that approval/acceptance will be, if you can get it. Again, this all comes back to a question of how much value you have with the other person. In most cases, assuming you have that value by teasing them a little will make them believe that you have value. Just remember not to flinch. Remember from "Questions vs. Statements" that you want to speak as if you already know them. The same is true for teasing. If done properly right from the get-go, it can make people feel as if they have known you longer than they actually have. If done wrong, they may feel like they have hated you for longer than they have known you.

How much is too much? Again, this is more of an art than a science. I'll remind you that if in the end they are smiling, you are doing it right. The guideline I go by is their perceived self-value. If I am talking to a girl at a bar who has had guys throwing themselves at her all night, I may say, "So do you owe it all to Nutrisystem?" If I say that to a fat girl sitting in the corner by herself, I am being a complete asshole and should be shot. Back in the day of selling computer technology, if I was quoting AT&T, I might say something in the meeting such as, "And I will be sure to list the professional-grade racking system along with the cheaper solution by Fisher-Price since I know you guys like to cut corners sometimes." This was my way of saying don't bitch about the cost of doing it right. I would never have said something like this to a smaller client because I knew I might run the risk of insulting him. The more self-perceived value the other person has, the more room you have to play with.

Keep in mind that if you ever find yourself at the point where you cannot get a girl to smile, you have lost the game. It helps to have a few fail-safe lines for when you blow it. My two favorites from years gone by are listed below.

Me: You couldn't afford the padded bra that at least fools drunk guys?

Her: [Ready to scratch my eyes out.]

Me: Quick. What movie is that from?

Me: Rookies! That was it.

Her: [No clue what is going on.]

When you say something that doesn't land right, make it sound as if you are just quoting some stupid movie. As a side note, you are never in danger of someone saying, "I don't remember that being in that movie." At the time of writing this, there is no movie with the title *Rookies*, so you are safe. The best part is that *Rookies* sounds like a movie you may vaguely remember watching on some crappy cable station at 3:00AM, but not quite. I have even had people reply to this one with, "Oh yeah." People will go along with *anything* to be part of the group, even if they have to pretend that they watched a movie that they don't know doesn't exist. People are silly.

Me: What are you, retarded?

Her: No, my sister is, though.

Me: Oh, I'm sorry. Sometimes I overdo the
        teasing. It's just how I grew up. All of us
        kidded around constantly as a sign of
        affection, and I was the youngest. I think I
        kind of got it the worst… [And lead the
        conversation to a new topic from when you
        were a kid.]

As I have said before, I make mistakes all the time, but that is how I have learned everything I know. Never be cruel to people and, as a general rule, leave them with a higher self-perceived value than you met them with. The goal in the end is that everyone is laughing.

Topics Never to Joke About

The core of humor is approval. When people ask you questions and you use humor in your answer, you have to understand that you are doing so to help get their approval with your answer. For this reason, it becomes easy for a person to hide behind humor. People who are constantly seeking approval are doing so because of their self-perceived low value. People who are constantly seeking to make people laugh are doing so because of their self-perceived low value. Being funny is one thing. Constantly seeking approval from others is another. Learn to be funny without needing laughter from people.

For this reason, never be evasive or use humor regarding your self-perceived shortcomings, whether they be sexual experience, height, money, or anything else. Most people know that you're bleeding inside when you smile too much. Now did I say never make jokes about your sexual experience, height, or wealth? Nope. I said that you should not make jokes about anything that you are uncomfortable with regarding yourself. Eventually, you should be able to joke about anything regarding yourself because you are so confident and sure of your core self-value that you are not using humor as a shield. Everyone has one or two things such as this with themselves. You know yours.

Stop hiding behind laughter and come to terms with these things. What you will find out is that the more personal you feel your shortcomings are, the more common you will find them to be. Remember the stubbing your toe example? Find someone like you, exchange stories, and have a good laugh about it. This is how things come full circle. Laughter in that case becomes self-acceptance, and then you move on.

Comedic victims build an identity out of their problems and never let go because that's how they get just that little bit of approval that keeps them going. Naturally humorous people have let go and have no problem laughing at their old misperceptions because they know they have core value right now.

Laughing at Your Own Jokes

Everyone assumes that you would approve of whatever you are saying. This is why laughing at your own jokes is a little off. Don't get me wrong. You are the number one person you should be focused on amusing. However, it's far better to get the sequence of events correct. Don't laugh at what you said; rather, laugh at people's reaction to what you said (whatever that may be). It's better to err on the more subdued side and then join in once they start laughing. This is more like giving them acceptance for giving you acceptance. If no one is laughing with you, find new friends. Life is far too short to be around people who do not share your sense of humor.

Self-Deprecating Humor

As a general rule, never use self-deprecating humor. The basic concept has a fatal flaw. Most people who use self-deprecating humor do it because it is an easy way to make others feel good about themselves. The problem is that use of self-deprecating humor gives value to people at the expense of removing value from yourself. As a general rule, you never want to do anything that lowers your value. The other problem with self-deprecating humor surfaces when you have lowered your value to the point where you have no more value to give. It is much smarter to get and maintain high value and simply bring everyone up to your level.

I say "as a general rule" above because, as with every other piece of advice I have given you, and will ever give you, it has exceptions. True social mastery is being able to get away with anything, and once you've mastered this, you will sometimes find that lowering your value momentarily will actually help serve your purpose.

There is no sport better than hunting perfect 10s at a Las Vegas nightclub. My favorite part of that game is that they are never alone. They continuously have guys throwing themselves at them, usually a few at a time. Each guy will do the same thing. He will walk up and attempt to show her that he has enough value to be with her. Every guy makes this same mistake of basically admitting to her that he is not good enough for her. I do it differently. I look her right in the eyes as I walk very directly toward her and through them, as if I were her older brother. I am completely ignoring everything else that is going on; only her eyes are relevant to me. I put my arm around her and whisper the following in her ear: "I have to say that one of my favorite things about a packed nightclub is that I can fart anytime I want and no one ever knows it's me." She laughs and I'm in. If only the other guys knew what I said, they would probably laugh also.

This works because this girl is used to every guy walking up to her and trying to prove his value. She sees this and realizes that, by their actions, they admit to not being good enough for her. They have something to prove. When I walked up to her and gave some of my value away, I showed her that I didn't care what she thought. This showed her that I think I have at least as much (if not more) value than she does. Will this line work for you? Probably not. Not until you truly believe at your core that you do, in fact, have more value than a perfect 10 in a Las Vegas nightclub.

At that point you could say anything and get away with it, just as I did.

I was attempting to lift the spirits of a student who had just blown his first big business deal. I heard the words, "But you don't know what it feels like. I was just so stupid." I knew at that point I was going to have to step off of my guru pedestal for a moment if I wanted to be able to help him. I told him the story of my first attempted deal in CPU chips. It started so well. I had a seller with product and a low price. I had a buyer who needed product and was willing to pay quite a bit more than what I was getting it for. The best part was the large quantity ordered. The deal had one condition. The buyer wanted a sample of ten units to test before accepting the full order. I delivered ten test units and waited for his call to deliver the rest. While I was waiting for the call, I was dreaming about how I was going to spend all of the money I was about to get. That was when I got the call. One of the units tested bad, and I lost the entire order. FUCK DAMN IT! In that instant, it occurred to me that I could have easily had the chips independently tested before I delivered them to him. I was so blinded by the thought of money that it never occurred to me to ensure I was delivering good product. If I had caught the bad part, it would have been very easy to have my vendor replace it. I was stupid. Lesson learned. My next deal went better.

Sometimes the social gap needs to be bridged. Sometimes the only way to get rapport with people is to lower yourself a little as you bring them up so you can meet in the middle. Sometimes showing them that you are human is the only way to do this. It's your humanity that makes for the most interesting stories.

What's Funny?

Everyone knows that the answer to the question "what's funny?" depends on who you ask. I am going to conclude with a very important concept. Only your opinion on this question matters. No other person's opinion on this question matters. *NO OTHER PERSON'S!* Laughter is approval, and you never need someone else's approval. All the funniest people I know don't care if other people find them funny, as long as they are having a good time. You will remember from my previous writings that the less you seek approval, the easier it is to get. Well, the less you seek laughter out of people, the more easily you will get it. Stay focused on what you find funny. Over time, you will use your humor as a kind of screening system to find people who are compatible with you. Not everyone will laugh at your jokes, and that is a good thing. Be yourself to the extreme, and you will find others like you. Pretend to be someone else, and you can pretend that the friends you make in that way would still like you if they knew who you really were. There are over seven billion people on this planet. Find the ones who share your sense of humor, and your life will improve dramatically.

Power Communication Part 8
Congruency

Week 8

Some people wonder what they are capable of while others take action and find out. For those who think something's impossible, they will prove themselves to be correct. For those who think something's possible, they to will prove themselves to be correct. With the precision of an equation, the outcome of any event will always be congruent with your thoughts and actions. Over time, you will ultimately accomplish either success or failure, all by your own design. You are about to learn that success is nothing more than a logical progression of events as you are 100% congruent with an idea.

Sifu parted the ropes for me. He pushed the bottom ones down with his left foot and raised the top ones with his hands. As I entered the kickboxing ring through the space he created for my first amateur full-contact fight, I remember the surge of adrenalin. At that point, it was as if something in me turned off and at the same time something else in me turned on and replaced it. What had turned off was all thinking and emotion. There was no internal dialog asking if I was ready for this. There was no doubt. There was no fear. The only thing that remained was my intent, and it

*was living through a primal instinct. It felt
unlimited and pure. I think it was the first time in
my life that I was truly alive and fully conscious.*

*I blame Karl. As with most of the things in my
life that I've done and wondered how exactly I got
to doing them, I blame Karl. When I met Karl, I
was a professional computer geek, and I lived most
of my life in my own head. As for Karl, he was too
busy crashing motorcycles and having sex with
obscenely hot girls to spend much time in his head.
Karl knew how to be alive in the moment, how to
have fun, and, most importantly, how not to ruin
things by overthinking everything. His credo was
"Why not? Yeah so? It could be fun!" Over the
years of being around him, I came out of my shell
more and more until there was no shell left.*

*So yes, back to blaming Karl for all the fun
I've had and for being the reason I was in a
kickboxing ring. One day Karl found out that I did
martial arts and asked if I had ever competed.
When I said no, he asked how long I had been
practicing. I've been doing martial arts since I
was a kid. I got a very confused look back from
him. You see, I had never thought of competing
before because I just thought it wasn't "me." He
asked me what the point was in training then. The
way he looked at it, competing was the natural
progression for someone who had studied that*

long. He had a point. I'm not sure where my self-limiting thinking on this came from. That was the way Karl always looked at things, just going with the flow, with the natural progression of things.

This was also how he had succeeded in sleeping with so many women. Where I was trying to figure out how to have sex, he didn't have to think about it. For him, sleeping with amazing women was just a natural progression from hanging out with amazing women. He just did it. As I was struggling to understand, he asked me how I got so good with computers. I told him I just did it. I just kept on playing with them and that is how I know so much about them. He told me that was how he learned so much about women. He just started playing with them. It made sense to me, and for one of the first times in my life I turned off my limiting beliefs and just started on a path. I was going to become a full-contact fighter.

The next day at my dojo, I told Sifu that I wanted to compete and asked him what was involved. It was a long list, and I remember thinking to myself, "Wow, that sounds difficult." The strange thing was that two months later, I had been doing it for two months. My computer company was running itself, and my full-time job had become training. The only thing that stayed the same was my height, six-foot-one. Sure, I had been working out most of my life, but not like this. Most of the "food" I was eating was from a nutrition store. I was spending two hours lifting weights plus two hours at the dojo no less than five days a week. I was sleeping about eleven hours a day to give my body enough time to repair each night. The results made it all worth it. I was 225 pounds at about 8% body fat. I was bench pressing 315 pounds. I was one sexy beast. The thing that I found most interesting was that my brain was still telling me that I could not achieve this, even though I had. I'm glad I ignored my counterproductive thinking and just stayed on the process. Eventually my brain gave up and just admitted that anyone who did what I was doing would get the same results. The advertising department at Nike was onto something when they said, "Just do it."

As my first fight ended, I remember the official raising my hand and the joy of victory. Then I remember taking one step with my left foot and then completely collapsing as I put weight on my right foot. As the doctor was putting the half-cast on my foot, I was told that I hadn't completely broken it. You have got to love blind delusional confidence. I had no clue that I had hurt it until the fight was over. I didn't even care that much about it in the hospital. I think that was because the woman who put my half-cast on was adorable and gave me this "kickboxers are hot" look while she was working.

On my way home, I checked my voicemail. There was a message from Chrystal saying that she was coming over with some friends to use my hot tub. I was hopeful that she was bringing her equally hot friend Barbie, who coincidently looked just like a Barbie doll. When I got home, there were about 20 people there. One of them asked me why I was on crutches. My friend John explained to him that I had just gotten back from a fight. John then asked me, "If you're on crutches, how is the other guy? Is he still alive?" John had not heard the results of the fight yet. I laughed at his comment (approval).

Let's take a quick inventory. Life was good. I could bench press 315 pounds and had about 8% body fat. I had the respect of all the guys. Chrystal looked amazing in her tiny little bikini, and so did all of her girlfriends. Chrystal's bikini had a very patriotic stars-and-stripes theme that I will never forget, because it was so small that it only had enough room for about three-and-a-half stars and two stripes. There was the little issue of my foot, but I proceeded to self-medicate for pain, because after all, it was a party. The pain went away, but the glory still lives on to this day.

Most people live their lives crippled by doubt. Their conflicting thoughts and conflicting actions are left uncontrolled and do nothing more than scatter their energy. They never really accomplish anything because for every thought or action that pushes them towards something, they have a thought or action that pulls them away from it. The ability to accomplish comes from congruency. When all of your thoughts and actions are toward a single goal, you are being congruent. Total congruency is true power in action. Those who keep on changing their destination will do nothing more than wander around in circles and will never get anywhere. Those who are congruent will find themselves in a constant state of action toward what they have decided they will have. For them it is never a question of if but rather a question of when. The more congruent they are, the sooner it will happen. For these reasons, all persuasive communication requires congruency. Problems with congruency can be seen whenever a person acts out of character for who they believe they are. The solution is found in the fact that beliefs can be changed.

In this final part of the book, I'm going to teach you about how your brain works. Then, like a computer programmer, you will take control of your own thoughts. You will then see that by mastering your thinking, you take control of reality itself.

The Function of Doubt

Why do we have doubt? If there were not some evolutionary advantage to having it 40,000 years ago, we would not have doubt today. Why can't we just walk around all of the time with our mojo flowing? Doubt is a protection mechanism. The fact that it cripples you from doing certain things is what keeps you alive. You could be 100% totally congruent in your belief that you can fly, but if you step off the side of a 20-story building, you will not have that belief very long. The problem isn't that your doubt system exists. The problem is that the software in your head that runs it, and runs everything else in you, is about 40,000 years out of date. That is approximately how long it takes evolution to catch up, so to speak.

Think of it like this. Let's say that you want to quit your advertising job and start your own advertising company. For some reason, you have this unexplainable fear in your head that keeps you from doing it. It's almost as if you feel your possible failure could result in death. It's completely irrational when you think about it, isn't it? Come on now, really, what is the worst that could happen? You may run out of money and have to find another job working for someone? OK, so you are back to square one. Big deal.

Think about this for a moment, logically. What if right now you lost everything? What if all of your money, possessions, and job were completely gone in an instant? Would you die? Nope. In fact, going through something like that could be one of the best experiences of your life, because you would realize how unimportant all that stuff really is. So where does this doubt and intense emotional fear come from? It comes from 40,000 years ago.

Your unconscious brain is not running software from today. It doesn't know what an advertising company is. It gets forced to replace the world of today with references from 40,000 years ago as it attempts to make sense of things and give you direction. Here is how your unconscious brain gets told the above story:

Let's say that you want to leave your small hunting tribe and start your own tribe. Once you leave, the leader of your old tribe will never let you back in. If you fail at starting your own tribe, you will actually die. Unless you are 100% sure you can successfully start your own tribe, the risk of certain death is not worth it. Your unconscious then puts this intense fear in you because it thinks that the fear will stop you. It is trying to keep you alive.

Your unconscious is always trying to help you. The problem is that it has a hard time figuring out what is actually taking place in today's environment. You must learn to use your logical brain to overcome the outdated programming of your unconscious. Evolution has actually built a mechanism to help you with this task also. When you use your logical brain to overcome your unconscious and are successful, you get rewarded with happy chemicals in your brain. This is your evolutionary incentive to logically get past your fears.

> *Jump out of an airplane. Right before you do, your unconscious will tell you, "Jump and die." Your unconscious doesn't understand the concept of a parachute because they didn't exist 40,000 years ago. When you make it safely to the ground, your unconscious will be very confused, your logical brain will have won, and you will have all kinds of happy natural chemicals in your brain as a reward. This reward serves as an incentive to logically figure out what else your unconscious may be wrong about.*

As you start playing with this concept, you will find out that you are capable of all kinds of things that you never even knew you had inside of you. The person who never pushes past fear has no idea what he is capable of. The person who pushes past fear finds out that there exists inside of him a complete set of instructions for performing tasks he never thought he could do. This is a very difficult concept for people who have not experienced it firsthand to understand. This instruction set is held by your unconscious mind, but it is also your unconscious mind that hides these instructions from you. Believe it or not, it does both for your own good.

Let's go back to the example above of you starting your own advertising company and how your unconscious sees that as starting your own hunting tribe. I will show this example as if your conscious and unconscious were having a conversation with each other.

Conscious: I want to leave my job and start my own advertising company.

Unconscious: If we leave our tribe, they will never let us back in, and we will die when we are most likely unsuccessful. Yup, we are going to either starve to death or get killed by a tiger when we have no one to help protect us. Very bad idea!

Conscious: I am doing it anyway.

Unconscious: Can't you feel this fear? This is me
                telling you that we are going to die.
                OK, fine. Here is even more fear.
                How about now? Do you still feel
                like this is a good idea? Don't kill us.

Conscious: Here I go. I am doing it.

Unconscious: OK, that is the last straw. I warned
                you. Here, feel this. This is crippling
                fear. Turn back now while we still
                can.

Conscious: I just handed in my resignation.

Unconscious: We are going to die.

Conscious: I feel good for having the balls to do
                that.

Unconscious: Well since there is no turning back
                now, I'd better show you everything
                we know about how to start a tribe.

Conscious: What!?! We know things about how
                to get a business going?

Unconscious: Sure. All those years of watching
                others run tribes. I was paying
                attention to everything. I remember
                all of it.

Conscious: What?!? You have been writing an instruction manual this entire time and you didn't tell me about it?

Unconscious: Yes.

Conscious: Why the hell didn't you tell me that we knew how to do this?

Unconscious: If you knew about all of the instructions I hide from you, there would be no limit to the stupid stuff you would try, and you would kill us in no time.

Conscious: OK, but I have just one more question.

Unconscious: What's that?

Conscious: Why would you take the time to create all of these instruction sets if you never want to share them with me?

Unconscious: Because if I didn't have them, you really would kill us when you do stupid stuff like this.

There you have it. These are the two biggest secrets that your unconscious has been hiding from you. Your unconscious will use fear to protect you right up to the point when you are actually doing something. If you can get past the fear through action, your unconscious will then help you in ways you never expected. When you fully understand this, your life will completely change. I know; you are very upset at your unconscious. I was too when I found this out.

Triune Brain Model

We previously discussed the human brain in terms of left and right hemispheres. Now let's discuss the triune brain model, which is an evolutionary way of looking at the brain. The human brain actually consists of three brains, with the second having grown on top of the first and the third having grown on top of the second. Each one of these separate brains has its own way of working and reason for existing. The three sections are the reptilian brain, the mammalian brain, and the higher-logic brain.

The reptilian brain includes the brain stem and, on the evolutionary timeline, it's the oldest section. It controls instinctive survival behavior. It is also responsible for controlling the muscles, balance, and autonomic functions such as breathing and heartbeat.

The mammalian brain grew over the reptilian brain and is the source of emotions. This section controls such things as feelings, memories, and the habits they create. It works on a system of emotion to create memories. When you smell fresh-baked chocolate chip cookies and all of a sudden remember a time in your grandmother's kitchen as a child, your mammalian brain is responsible. Everything in this part of your brain works inside of a context of something being either agreeable or disagreeable. Within the mammalian brain, survival becomes a game based on the avoidance of pain (disagreeable) and seeking the reoccurrence of pleasure (agreeable).

The newest section is the higher-logic brain, also known as the cerebral cortex. This section is responsible for higher-order thinking skills such as reason and speech. If I ask you to figure out the square root of 37, this is the part of your brain you use.

The older the section is on the evolutionary timeline, the more dominant it is. To test this, simply hold your breath as long as you can. When you do this, you are creating an argument between your higher-logic brain and your reptilian brain, and your reptilian brain will eventually win. This older-section hierarchy of dominance explains why it is hard to use reason (least dominant = higher-logic brain) with people in a very emotional state (more dominant = mammalian brain), yet no matter what emotional state they are in, touching a hot stove will always produce the same reaction of pulling their hand away (most dominant = reptilian brain). Sometimes these separate brains conflict, as is the case when you really want to do something but know you shouldn't. Sometimes these separate brains have trouble communicating, as is the case when you suddenly realize how hungry you are. Hunger is generated in the reptilian brain, but awareness happens outside of that brain. So the awareness of hunger involves the separate brains working together.

When you understand the brain as these three separate and different sections attempting to work together, you understand the origins of personal internal conflict. As humans, we can use our cerebral cortex to understand the rules that run the entire system. When we understand the rules, we can then properly use the system to our advantage. Ideally we want to put our logical brain in charge of the other two sections. It may be the weakest, but it's also the smartest, and that fact is what makes our goal achievable.

Emotion and Memory

Let's look deeper into how the mammalian brain functions. This part of your brain helps you to remember things by attaching emotion to the memories. Think about your childhood. First, I want you to remember your most painful memory from before your tenth birthday. Second, I want you to remember your happiest memory from before your tenth birthday. Now, from that same time period, I want you to remember something that had zero emotion attached to it. Try hard. You cannot do the last one, can you? Anything you remember from before the age of 10 has at least some emotion attached to it. That is how you remember it. As for the first two memories, I know that your most painful and happiest memories are very strong. The stronger the emotion, the stronger the memory. Your mammalian brain figures that if something didn't generate emotion, it's not worth remembering. The happier it made you or the more it hurt you, the more valuable it must be to remember.

When you were a small child, you learned how to put your hands out in front of yourself to break your fall. At some point before you learned this, you fell on your face, and it hurt, a lot. That pain built a memory. The pain reminded you that you did not want to fall on your face again and that it

hurt far less to use your hands to break your fall,
rather than breaking it with your face. This is a
memory reinforced by pain.

When you were a small child and you tasted
candy for the first time, it was very yummy. That
very yummy and pleasurable taste built a memory.
The next time your eyes noticed a piece of candy,
you remembered how yummy candy was, and you
fidgeted to get more. This is a memory reinforced
by pleasure.

The next thing to understand is that memories are
state-based. The emotional state you are in at a specific
time dictates what memories you have access to at that
time. To understand this, we will look at how a
doughnut could remind you of a pair of socks.

Do you remember putting on a pair of socks
from over a week ago? How about just a few days
ago? OK, how about the last time you put on a
pair of socks? What do you remember about it? If
you are like most people, you don't remember
much about the actual putting on of the socks. You
are most likely to remember it in a way that
resembles this: "Well, I have socks on now, so yes,
I must have put them on at some point [logical].
Let me think for a moment. Oh yeah, I put them on
while sitting on my bed!" And if I were to ask

which foot a sock was put on first, most people would have to think for a second, and they would not be totally sure of their answer. If you had a gun to your head and your life depended on getting that answer correct, how sure would you be? If I were to ask you the same question about socks from over a week ago, you would have no clue because the memory has faded. The reason for this memory loss is that putting on a pair of socks is usually a boring and unemotional event. It's like brushing your teeth every morning. You know you do it, but it's so boring that you don't remember much unless something eventful happens while you are doing it.

Now for a moment consider the following: What if one day, while you were putting on a pair of socks, you had an instantaneous orgasm for no reason. Let's say that this happened to you five years ago. That memory would be with you for the rest of your life because it's odd and full of emotion. In fact, even if your socks all look exactly the same, you could probably tell me details about the pair you were putting on that day. For example, you would remember the one on your left foot having a little hole above the heel. You would pay close attention so you could identify the pair later to put them on the same feet in the same way, all in an attempt to duplicate the same outcome. This is your mammalian brain at work.

So now let's say that 10 years later, you were at a friend's house, and he had some doughnuts in the kitchen. As you bit into one, you had an instantaneous orgasm. The first image to enter your brain (as soon as the pleasure juice stopped flowing) would be a pair of socks. How interesting is that!?! Well, maybe not as interesting as having an orgasm from biting into a doughnut, but I think you get my point. And what would you do next? You would start telling the story to your friend, whose complete attention you would no doubt have.

Remembering that pair of socks was based on the state you were in with the doughnut. The stronger the emotion, the stronger the memory. When you duplicate the emotional state, you get access to the memories created in that state. This is why women tend to remember more details of a first date, and for a longer time, than a man would. Women tend to be more emotional.

Anchoring

When I was a toddler, I had an orange plastic toy screwdriver. Some children had a blankie. Some had a pacifier. I had an orange screwdriver. I was a strange child. From an early age, I wasn't interested in cuddling or sucking on things as much as I was in taking things apart. I was a terror on earth when I got my first Swiss Army knife. Anyway, when you're a toddler, you have that one item that has an almost magical power to it. It's your favorite thing on earth. For whatever reason, you have decided this item makes everything OK, as long as you are holding it. It is as if good emotions are somehow linked, or anchored, to that item.

The term *anchoring* is from Neuro-Linguistic Programming. An anchor is created when our brain associates an emotion with an item or event. Anchoring is very powerful and is one of the core ways a human learns. The next story illustrates how an anchor gets built.

Harvey and Teresa have never met. Harvey is your average guy, and Teresa is incredibly attractive. They both live in New York City. One day they are walking toward each other in Central Park. Harvey notices Teresa. She is wearing a green dress. Teresa walks up to him without saying a word and starts kissing him passionately. This lasts for 30 seconds, and then she runs away. The next day, they meet again in the same place at the same time. This time however, Teresa is wearing a red dress. Teresa walks up to him without saying a word, kicks him in the balls, and runs off. Because of the strong and confusing emotions Harvey is feeling, he returns to the park the following day, at the same place and same time. Teresa is wearing a green dress again. Harvey, protecting himself this time, waits for her approach. Teresa walks up to him, and as he is asking her name, she starts kissing him passionately for one minute. She then immediately runs away while saying, "My name is Teresa!"

So what does Harvey do? He shows up the next day, but she doesn't. Now Harvey is what we call obsessed. He keeps on showing up every day until he sees her again four days later. She is wearing a red dress and kicks him in the balls.

Now if Harvey's logical brain would kick in for a second, he would stop going to the park, but you guessed it, he keeps going back. Over the next six weeks Harvey goes to the park almost every day. Teresa is randomly there about once a week.

Every time she is in a green dress, she kisses him.
Every time she is in a red dress, she tries to attack
him. At least by this point, Harvey has become
smart enough that as soon as he sees her in a red
dress, he runs away.

One day Teresa shows up in a blue dress.
Harvey is paralyzed by a sense of fear and
excitement. He has no idea what is going to
happen. She walks past him as if he is not even
there. The following day, he sees her again. She is
wearing a green dress. She walks up to him and
kicks him in the balls. Harvey stops going to the
park. Every time after that, whenever Harvey sees
a girl in a green dress, he remembers that crazy
bitch Teresa.

The above is an extreme example of how anchors
get built. Anchor-building happens all of the time, and
usually you are completely unaware that it is even
going on. Let's go back to talking about socks. Do you
remember Lena, the one I met at the Cheesecake
Factory in Newport Beach as she was having dinner
with her family? If you do, it's because that story
invoked emotion in you, and those emotions help you
remember it.

The following Easter after meeting her, she did
the coolest thing a girl had ever done for me up to

301

that point in my life. She got me an Easter basket. I hadn't gotten one of those since I was a young kid. I remember the huge smile she had on her face as she brought it out. I also remember the basket being almost bigger than she was. Lena was 23 years old but only five feet tall and 98 pounds. At first I thought it was just a big Easter basket that she picked up at a Kmart or someplace like that. As I got a closer look at it, I realized that she had purchased the basket and items separately. It had some of the normal stuff in it such as candy and the obvious chocolate bunny, but it was the other items that almost got me to propose to her on the spot (no joke). Still to this day, I cannot believe what she had done.

She had taken the time to drive all over Southern California, back to each place we had been together. For each date we had been on, she went back for a souvenir, about a half-dozen items total. One of the items was a pair of socks I showed her while we were in a store called Hot Topic at the Irvine Spectrum Center. They were black with the pirate skull and crossbones on them.

This is my "Anchor Basket Story." What did Lena give me? It wasn't just an Easter basket; it was a basket of emotions. That pair of socks was one of the anchors.

Whenever I put them on, I would feel all happy inside. To this day, whenever I see a pirate skull-and-crossbones image, I feel a little of what I felt when she gave me that Easter basket.

The next thing to understand is that most anchors apply to multiple events, all with a slightly different (or sometimes totally different) emotional content and possibly conflicting instruction sets. Consider the pirate skull-and-crossbones image for me. One time I was a pirate for Halloween, and that event has its own childhood emotions and memories associated with it. Then there is the Pirates of the Caribbean ride at Disneyland. The last time I was on that, I was on a date with an amazing blonde named Ashley. That fact reminds me that I've seen all the *Pirates of the Caribbean* movies... and so on, and so on. For me, the pirate skull-and-crossbones image has many different life experiences attached to it, but I tend to remember Lena first because my memories about her have the strongest emotions attached to them. For most anchors, there are usually multiple connections. The connection with the strongest emotion tends to be the one that you remember first and controls you the most.

As children, we learn that falling and landing on our face hurts. That process has only negative emotions attached to it. As a result, we learn to do everything in our power to avoid that situation.

As for my orange screwdriver, it had only positive emotions attached to it. The result was that whenever I held it, I felt good.

If we consider our poor friend Harvey, his "green dress" anchor has a massive and equal amount of positive and negative emotional charge to it. For him, this anchor creates nothing but massive internal conflict.

Falling on your face hurts. Holding an orange screwdriver makes me feel good. Seeing a hot girl in a green dress drives Harvey to dysfunctional insanity. It's not a perfect system, and more so than you might ever comprehend, a person's "choice and free will" are nothing more than the products of this system. Your mammalian brain is doing its best to guide you toward pleasure and away from pain. Sometimes this system fails and actually hurts you more than it helps.

Superstitions and Self-Fulfilling Prophecies

One of the possible failures of the mammalian brain is the generation of superstitions and self-fulfilling prophecies. Remember that this section of the brain makes emotional decisions, not logical ones. Therefore, it is possible for it to guide you in an illogical manner if it decides it's moving you away from pain or towards pleasure.

The brain is an incredible tool. Presented with any question, it will give the best answer possible. That's its job, to figure stuff out. The problem is that in the absence of scientific and factual data, it has a tendency to make shit up. This is the downside of an imagination. If you didn't know the structure of our solar system and grew up by yourself on a desert island, you too may very well come up with a "god concept" and think it is the hand of your god concept that pushes the sun up out of the ocean every morning. The reason for this is simple. It is better for you to recognize the pattern of the sun rising every morning (and be wrong about why) than not to see the pattern at all. As soon as your brain notices the pattern, it starts working to answer the question why. Your brain knows that your survivability increases as you understand more and more of your environment.

A superstition is an irrational belief arising from ignorance or fear. A superstition must have an emotional charge and a lack of logic to survive. A superstition is deconstructed to nonexistence by removing emotion and engaging logic. In most cases, religious believers consider the beliefs of other religions to be superstitious. Likewise, atheists regard all religious belief as superstition. Anything that you do out of fear (that lacks a logical reason) needs to be logically evaluated in the absence of emotion. It's time to free yourself. Some call it religion, but I see it as organized superstition, and I know of no easier method to get good people to do bad things.

> *"Is God willing to prevent evil, but not able? Then he is not omnipotent. Is he able, but not willing? Then he is malevolent. Is he both able and willing? Then whence cometh evil? Is he neither able nor willing? Then why call him God?"*
>
> *- Epicurus (ancient Greek philosopher)*

A self-fulfilling prophecy is a prediction that directly or indirectly causes itself to become true. It starts off with a logically false assumption based in emotion. This assumption then sufficiently influences people so that their reactions ultimately fulfill the false prophecy. A self-fulfilling prophecy is deconstructed to nonexistence by redefining the propositions on which its false assumptions are originally based. Below is one that I discovered in myself a few years ago.

For some reason, I don't like blonde girls with brown eyes. It just doesn't look right to me. The odd thing is that I have had a large number of really amazingly hot blonde girls with brown eyes chase me over the years. My false assumption and self-fulfilling prophecy was that all hot blonde girls with brown eyes were attracted to me.

Here is where I was wrong. The true equation was actually very simple. When I would see an attractive blonde girl who knew how hot she was, I would look at her with a certain "you can't have me" disapproval. Because she was used to all of the guys chasing her, she would become interested in what she could not have (as I said, it only happened with the very attractive ones). She would chase me. Sooner or later, I would give in. OK, maybe I wasn't a fan of blonde hair and brown eyes, but these girls were so hot that I eventually looked past my silly preference to enjoy other areas of their bodies.

Socially Learned Behaviors

One of the great things about being human is that we can learn from those around us. We do not need to fully understand what others know to benefit from that understanding. Think about flying in an airplane. Do you need to understand how it works to get from LA to Chicago in one? Nope. We tend to adopt a socially learned behavior when following that behavior has benefit to us. In the case of an airplane, we do what others do to get the same benefits as they have. If you look at the warning labels on household cleaning supplies, you may see something warning you not to mix products containing chlorine bleach with products containing ammonia because it will kill you. You don't need to understand why; you just need to know that the last time a person did this it ended very badly. The law works in the same way. Society says that the speed limit on a certain street is 45 miles per hour. If you get caught doing 75, you are going to experience pain as delivered via a police officer. The problem is that humans are imperfect. Sometimes what you learn from others may seem to be of benefit to you when in fact it is detrimental. The next example shows just how wrong things can go.

Start with a cage containing five monkeys. In the cage, hang a banana from the ceiling on a string, and put stairs under it. Before long, a monkey will go to the stairs and start to climb toward the banana.

As soon as he touches the stairs, spray all of the monkeys with cold water.

After a while, another monkey will make an attempt with the same result. All of the monkeys are sprayed with cold water. Keep this up for several days.

Disable the cold water sprayers.

Later, if another monkey approaches the stairs, the other monkeys will attack him to prevent cold water from spraying on them even though the cold water sprayers have been disabled.

Now, remove one monkey from the cage and replace it with a new one.

The new monkey sees the banana and wants to climb the stairs. To his horror, all of the other monkeys attack him as he gets close. After another attempt and attack, he knows that if he tries to climb the stairs, he will be assaulted.

Next, remove another one of the original five monkeys and replace it with a new one. The newcomer goes to the stairs and is attacked. The previous newcomer takes part in the punishment with enthusiasm.

Replace the third original monkey with a new one. The new one makes it to the stairs and is attacked as well. Two of the four monkeys that beat him have no idea why they were not permitted to climb the stairs or why they are participating in the beating of the newest monkey.

After replacing the fourth and fifth original monkeys, all the monkeys that have been sprayed with cold water have been replaced. Nevertheless, no monkey ever again approaches the stairs.

Why not?

"Because that's the way our society does things."

Again, logic is the answer. Learn to question the logic behind everything you see in society. If people cannot give you a logical answer, think twice before duplicating their actions.

Pain as Pleasure and Pleasure as Pain

In some cases, the mammalian brain can fail to the point of rewarding you for bad things and punishing you for good things. In the absence of logic, anything is possible. To some mentally ill people, purposefully cutting themselves and watching the blood flow creates a positive. They have so lost touch with reality that the pain is the only thing that is real to them anymore. To a religious person, the beauty of a sexual relationship is killed by guilt because ultimately they feel believing so is for the better. All addictions are attributable to this failure in the brain, because addiction without emotion is impossible.

Positive emotions make life worth living, while negative emotions can help keep us alive. Emotions outside of the fail-safe system of logic can destroy life itself. All the wars that have ever been fought on our planet have their roots in only one war: the war of logic versus emotion. When logic has won over emotion inside of the head of every man, woman, and child on our planet, that war, and all wars, will end. This is the evolution of the human race.

Intermission Time

This is a great place to take a break in your reading and let your head cool off a bit. Please take an intermission, even if you just took one a few minutes ago. When you return, we will go yet another level deeper.

Time Doesn't Exist

That's right, time doesn't exist. Now you understand why I told you to take a break before reading further. The concept you hold in your head called *time* is actually a construct built by your brain (and everyone else's) to understand our environment. Like all of the maps of reality you hold in your head, it has its flaws. Now I can almost hear the people reading this for the first time saying, "But I know time is real because I can experience it!" Just like Billy Graham, who is sure that god is real because he can experience it, it's all in your head. As they said in one of my favorite movies, *The Matrix* (1999), "Your brain makes it real." And just as in the movie, if I can get you to see the Matrix for what it really is, I can then teach you how to hack the system, to make it into whatever you wish.

OK Neo, it's time to really pay attention here. The concept you hold in your head called *time* has three sections. It's like a filing cabinet with three drawers. Everything can be put into one of the three drawers. Because your brain cannot deal with everything at once, it uses the time filing system to keep things manageable and, when things change, it moves the files around. The three drawers are History, Now, and Future. History is for things that have already happened. Now is for things that are currently happening. Future is for things that have not happened yet. Here is where this construct falls apart...

When you think about history, when do you do it? Now. When you think about the future, when do you do it? Now. The only time that you can think about history or the future is now. In fact, right now is the only time you can do anything. Your perception of history can be accomplished only in the present moment. As for your predictions of the future, these also can only be accomplished in the present moment. The future never actually happens. We are always in the present moment. **When** do the past and the future exist? At the only time it can: right now. **Where** does the past and future exist? The only place it can: in your head.

Am I saying that a cause-and-effect relationship doesn't exist in the universe? Not at all. What has happened affects Now, which in turn affects Future. I am not saying that the relationship doesn't exist. What I am saying is that our map of this relationship, which we know as time, is only a map. Time is not the relationship itself, only an imperfect map of it.

Let's examine the relationship. Our map called *time* is based on how long it takes the earth to go around our sun. It takes "one year" for that to happen. We further divide that "one year" into how many times the earth spins around its own axis and call those spins *days*. How many "days" in a "year?" There are 365 days in a year. But what about leap year? OK, so some years have 366 days. Doesn't our map seem a little imperfect if we have to correct it every now and then by adding February 29th? So let's get this straight then. It would seem that there are 365.25 days in a year because leap year happens every fourth year. Let's do a Google search for "how many days in a year" to get an exact answer. Google tells me that "1 year = 365.242199 days." OK, so it's an imperfect system, but at least now we have a solid and exact number. Or do we? A few results under that on the Google page, the US Military (www.cs.nps.navy.mil) tells me, "QUESTION: How Many Days in a Year? ANSWER: 365.24219878 (approximately)." Do they say "approximately" because they don't know, or could it be that the number is always changing? Are you starting to see my point yet? Oh yes, it gets better… (Now is a great time to take a Tylenol for the headache you're about to get.)

Most everyone has heard of leap years, but did you know there are also leap seconds? That's right, leap seconds. Look it up at www.wikipedia.com and be amazed. Here is how this happens. We use atomic clocks that work by timing the electrons spinning around the nucleus of an atom to tell us the "exact time." A certain number of orbits of the electrons = the orbit of the earth around the sun. It is a relative relationship. So many of this = so many of that. Here is the problem. The solar system is slowing down relative to the speed at which electrons are orbiting in atoms. Over longer and longer time periods, leap seconds must be added at an ever-increasing rate. The longer we use this system, the more screwed up it gets.

Einstein told us this. Everything is relative. There are no constants in the universe, only relative relationships. If everything in the universe suddenly slowed down to half speed (all at the exact same moment), we couldn't possibly know it because we wouldn't have anything running at the old speed to compare it to. Time exists only in our heads to explain an observed relative relationship. All time says is that "this object is here relative to this other object being there." When the hands on my watch were on the 3:00 position, I was at the mall. It is a map of reality but it is not reality itself. This map, like every other map, is imperfect.

The Map Is Not the Territory

It's April 2008 and I am in Tucson, Arizona. I have never been here before, but with the help of a GPS navigation system, I am good to go. GPS car navigation systems are just too cool. I can go wherever I want, with no clue how to get there. I just watch the map and follow the directions. I love it because with its help, I venture out and do all kinds of things I normally wouldn't do. In my opinion, it's one of the most useful things they have ever put in cars.

So I am on the 10 Freeway, and I see a barrage of orange construction signs. Some group of idiots at Tucson City Planning has decided to close about 20 exits in a row. Yes, all of them. During that planning meeting, no one apparently was smart enough to think that they might want to leave maybe at least one open exit in the middle somewhere. So I have my GPS, but my GPS has no idea that I am unable to exit the freeway until next Tuesday. After a few miles, I actually get annoyed with the GPS unit as it keeps on telling me that I missed an exit, followed by recalculating the route, followed by telling me that I missed another exit. The GPS unit must have thought I was retarded.

Once I could exit the freeway and get around the construction, the GPS unit did one more route recalculation, and I was back on track. The GPS is great, but it's not a perfect system. Sometimes you have to use logic to get the system back to where it can help you again. If I would have blindly followed the GPS, I would have driven straight into a concrete barrier at 80 mph.

Time Heals All Wounds

The saying is that time heals all wounds. It's not true. Time is not the process that heals the wounds, but the process that heals wounds usually does take time. The power in this is the realization that time is not needed to heal. The healing can be done without the time.

Most of the pain in this world doesn't actually exist. I know, first I told you time doesn't exist. Now I am telling you that most pain doesn't exist either (even though what I'm saying here has probably given you a headache). It's called reality deconstruction, and yes, it can be a little unsettling. Back to the point: most pain doesn't exist for the same reason that time doesn't exist. When do you feel pain? Now is the only time you can feel pain. To feel pain from the past, you must feel it now. To feel pain from the future that has not happened yet, you must also feel it now. Everything, including pain, can happen only now. Pain can only exist in the present moment. Now it is true that if you stub your toe, right now, you will feel real pain, right now. But pain in the present moment is never really that bad. I know you disagree with me on this because you "remember pain in the past as being bad." Let's shift your thinking, your logical thinking for a moment, to help you remember pain that was not that bad, and as such you have a hard time remembering it (this should all be starting to come together for you now).

Can you remember ever hitting your thumb with a hammer? What happened? You hit your thumb, and for a half second, you were not even sure if you actually did or not. Then what happened? As soon as you realized that you had, about a half second later, the pain started. Have you ever cut yourself with a knife? What happened? You cut yourself, and you may not have even been aware of it until you actually saw blood. Then what happened? As soon as you saw blood, about a half second later, the pain started.

When you remember pain moment by moment, you actually start to question how much it hurt in any specific moment. Inside of the first second, before your brain decides it hurts, it doesn't actually hurt at all, does it? After that it hurts, but how much? What really "hurts" is the memory. Your brain actually tends to exaggerate it to help you to remember not to do it again. How does it play this little trick on you?

Let's say, for ease of explanation, that your concept of now is a one-second window. Then let's say that you have a pain meter that you use to define your current state. It goes from 1–10, one being not much pain and ten being the worst pain possible, so bad that you lose consciousness from an overload of pain. You hit your thumb with a hammer; we give that a six. In that moment, you feel a six. When you remember that pain later, you do not remember it moment by moment. Your memory (in an attempt to remind you not to do that again) exaggerates it by adding the pain of the first second, to the pain of the second second, to the pain of the third second, and so on. Because you are remembering the sum of all the pain all at once, the memory of it is actually stronger than the six that actually happened moment by moment.

When you are remembering pain of the past, it can exist only in the present moment, and it is not real, but your brain makes it real.

The compounding of emotion through time works in the opposite forward direction also. When you feel pain from an anticipated future event, as is the case with worry, the pain exists only in your head, and your brain makes it real. When you worry about an event that has not happened yet, you live that painful moment over and over again in your head. Even though it may never even happen, you may have lived it in your head hundreds or even thousands of times. If your greatest fears do come to pass, reality only requires you live it once, in that moment.

How about pain in the present moment? How real is that? Stay with me here… that's all in your head also. It's as real as your brain tells you it is. As a certified clinical hypnotherapist, I can tell you that pain in the present moment can be turned off, depending on the concentration and willingness of the subject and the skill of the hypnotherapist. As a martial artist, I can tell you that most people have no clue as to the power that exists inside of their own minds, including the ability to stop pain.

Some people may choose to interject the philosophical argument here that the pain hasn't stopped, just the perception of the pain. This is the age-old question of "If a tree falls in the forest and no one is around to hear it, does it make a sound?" Let me answer that philosophical argument with another one. Does your pain really exist if you cannot feel it? How would you know, considering that no one else could feel it but you?

Perception = Reality

Perception is reality. Perception is relative. Is reality relative? Yes, it is. The Doppler effect demonstrates this scientific fact. It explains the change in frequency and wavelength of a wave as perceived by an observer moving relative to the source of the waves. Let me give you an example that makes this simple to understand.

Think about the last time a fire truck passed by you with its sirens on. As it approached you, the sirens had a higher pitch. Once it passed you, the sirens had a lower pitch. Your perception of the sound is relative to the speed and direction of the fire truck in relation to you. That same sound was an unchanging constant to the people on the fire truck when it passed you by. Therefore, reality was different for you than it was for the people on the fire truck.

The above example was with sound waves. Next we will look at an example with light waves.

Let's say that you and I are playing catch with a ball of green light. Let's say that we could throw that light very fast. Let's say that we could throw it so fast that the Doppler effect happened to the light waves the same way it happened to the sound waves as in our fire truck example above. What would happen? The light would change colors. When the light was still, it would be green. When the light was moving toward you, it would be blue. When the light was moving away from you, it would be red. The most interesting part however is that when it was blue for you, it would be red for me, and when it was red for you, it would be blue for me. Now I ask you, what color is the light? Is it red, green, or blue?

From the above examples, we see that perception is reality, and different perceptions can produce different realities.

The Perception of Existence

What is real? The classic popular answer to this question is "If I can see, smell, touch, taste, and/or hear it, it must be real." More evidence that perception is reality. We have one last concept to come to terms with before we can move on.

> *The game is called Connect the Dots. A child gets a piece of paper that is mostly empty space. This mostly empty space has small dots on it. Each dot has a number next to it. At first glance, there appears to be nothing on the page other than the apparently random scattering of the dots. When the child takes a pencil and draws straight lines connecting the dots according to the numbering sequence, a picture appears. Even thought the paper is over 99.9 % empty space, by "connecting the dots," a picture appears.*

This is exactly what happens with your perception of physical reality. Every object is well over 99.9% empty space. Whether it's water, a pencil, or your own body, everything is made up of atoms, and atoms are mostly empty space. To give you an illustration, if an atom were the size of a football stadium, the nucleus would be a fly in the middle, with the electrons orbiting the walls. You may think of a block of concrete as being solid, but in fact it's almost completely empty space. This is the illusion of physical reality. Take a moment and look at something in your environment right now and come to terms with the fact that over 99.9% of it is empty nothingness. Your reality is more the imaginary lines created by your brain to connect the dots than it is the dots themselves.

Acceptance

So where does that leave us? Reality deconstructed, that's where. Now that we have taken everything apart, we need to start putting things back together for the sake of your sanity. This is a dangerous point where some of my readers will start to wonder if they can walk through walls. If they try, all that will result is a bruise on the forehead. Pain is the result when people disagree with reality, and their mammalian brain will do its job in reminding them not to do it again.

Remember that the universe must operate under a set of equations that maintain balance. Without certain scientific laws, the universe would collapse and cease to exist. That would be bad. What I am telling you is that reality is like a game of Connect the Dots. Your power comes from realizing how much of your reality is in your head. Sure, at the core, there exist laws of the universe, which are the dots, but that's less than 1% of the picture. Argue with that less than 1% and you will lose every time. What we are working with is the other 99% that's all in your head. That is my greater point here. All of your limiting beliefs exist only in your head. They are not real, and they do you no good. It's time to upgrade the software in your brain.

How to Program the Human Brain

Congratulations are in order! Seriously, you've made it this far without your brain melting. We've come a long way from the abolishment of the word *try* and poop in the hand jokes of part one. Now that you understand some of the basic mechanics of how the human brain constructs reality and some of the inherent problems with the system, we can finally discuss how to make the system better.

Most people on this planet are going through life like a car driving down the freeway with its emergency brake on. They are not congruent. They are wasting their energy by fighting themselves. They are going much slower than their potential and tearing themselves up in the process. The power of congruency comes when every part of the system is synchronized as it puts energy toward the same goal. Over time, the momentum of this congruency becomes an unstoppable force.

When I was in school, I was a computer science major. I learned computer programming languages such as Turbo Pascal, C++, and LISP. A programming language was my way to give the computer instructions in the form of code that it could understand and use. The better my instructions were, the better the computer functioned to fulfill the task.

Your brain is just like a computer. In fact, it actually is a super-advanced neurobiological computer that can program itself. As we have discussed above, most of the programming that exists in your brain got there automatically, outside of your own conscious awareness. When we desire to consciously change the programming, we need a suitable programming language. One of the programming languages that can be used to program a brain is called Neuro-Linguistic Programming. As with any programming language, it has its imperfections, but in the hands of someone who knows how to use it, amazing things can be accomplished. We will now use the help of NLP to show you how to install better software inside of your own brain.

Replace Not Delete

Do not think of a pink elephant. Stop thinking about a pink elephant! No really, stop thinking about that mental picture you now have in your head of an all-pink elephant... it's not working, is it? Nope. Why? Because your brain has problems working with negatives. Guess what happens when you tell yourself, "Stop smoking?" The same thing. How about this one? "I don't want to be lonely!" None of this works. All self-reprogramming must be done in terms of positives.

> *If you walk into a dark room and I tell you to turn off the darkness, what happens? You cannot turn off the darkness. The only solution is to turn on the light. As an analogy, most of the people on this planet are running around trying to turn off the darkness. Silly people. There is no switch to turn off the darkness.*

Let's say that you have decided to lose weight. If you sit there and say, "I do not want to be fat," what are you doing? All you are accomplishing is the reinforcement that you are fat. You cannot "turn off the fat;" you have to "turn on the skinny." You have to give your body better options. One example would be in how you shop for food. As you shop, are you running the following program in your head? "Skinny people buy healthy food. I buy healthy food." Another program may be "Skinny people watch TV only while on a treadmill at the gym. I'd better get to the gym if I want to catch the beginning of my favorite TV show."

Your brain is simply amazing. No matter what thoughts you throw at it, it will work with that information and follow the path you have set it on. As an example, let's say that I ask a perfectly mentally healthy and happy individual, "If you were to kill yourself, how would you do it?" What happens? His brain starts looking for answers on how he could kill himself. This is how your brain works. Ask it a question, and it gives you an answer, but remember that it cannot understand questions phrased as a negative. Give it a statement, and it gives you more data to back that statement up, but remember that it cannot understand statements phrased as negatives. As an example of this, let's say I am with a clinically depressed person and ask her, "Do you remember that thing you said to me the other day? It made my day. I laughed so hard when I thought about it later." What happens? Her brain will start going through memories to find the most humorous interaction between the two of us. What happens if two days later I remind the happy person to stop thinking about suicide and the depressed person to stop thinking about how she made me laugh? In both cases, it's a negative command, and it has the opposite effect. Amusing, isn't it?

> *Jake and Jenna are "dating." Every time Jenna get's cranky with him, Jake tells her to "stop being a bitch!" The problem is that this is a negative statement. Jake has no clue as to what he is actually programming into her brain every time he says that. This statement is a presupposition. When you tell people to stop doing something, it presupposes that they are already doing it. Basically, every time Jenna is told to "stop being a bitch," the fact that she is "being a bitch" gets programmed into her brain. Sooner or later Jenna's ego will start building an identity from this, that she is "a bitch."*

"Stop being a bitch" can be just like asking a normal, happy person, "If you were to kill yourself, how would you do it?" You are using the power of suggestion to get his brain started down a path of bad thinking. If you want to have some fun testing this out, go through your day telling women to "stop being a bitch" in response to anything they do. And for however they reply to that comment, all you say in response is, "Just stop. It's not cute." As you do all this, be sure to look upset as you make these comments. You will find out that you can turn a perfectly happy woman into a bitch quickly and easily by simply telling her not to be a bitch. Once you see the power of suggestion in action, you will start making only positive presuppositions. Have fun with "stop being so nice to me." My favorite way to do this is when they give me "free bags" at the grocery store. "No, you are too kind. I do not deserve it." It can be quite ridiculous and a bunch of fun.

So what do you replace "stop being a bitch" with? Well, in the case of Jake, he is a cool guy who knows he has value, and knows he deserves a cool girlfriend. In fact, he is so congruent in his beliefs that it would be incongruent for him to be with a bitch. That's right; make sure you understand the path of congruency here. If Jake has value and deserves a cool girlfriend, it would be incongruent for him to make the statement "stop being a bitch" because it would imply that he is with a bitch.

THIS IS YOUR FIRST EXAMPLE OF COMMUNICATING CONGRUENTLY. THIS IS WHAT ALL OF THE PRECEDING INFORMATION IN THIS BOOK HAS BEEN LEADING UP TO. WELCOME TO THE WORLD OF REALITY BY DESIGN.

Jake cannot tell his girlfriend to stop being a bitch because that would imply that he is with a bitch and would only reinforce his own incongruency. The question then becomes, what would be congruent? Let's say that they are on their way to lunch. Jake suggests Mexican food. Jenna tells him that she hates Mexican food. Jake tells her, "That's why I love you so much though. You are so easygoing, adventurous, and up for new things. I think that's one of the reasons I choose to be with you." Keep in mind that he says this in a completely honest and sincere way, as he truly believes this. Now he is congruent and reinforcing positive behavior. This is an incredibly powerful combination. And if Jenna should disagree with him, the presupposition is that Jake will no longer be interested in spending time with her, but he will still be congruent and have no problem picking from one of the other girls waiting to spend time with him. Congruency forces reality.

Let's briefly return to the story about how Karl talked me into the inside of a kickboxing ring. How did this happen in terms of what we have been talking about? The first step was for me to throw out my limiting beliefs. It began with the realization that the only thing preventing me from kickboxing competitively was a set of thoughts I chose to hold inside my own head. I got rid of those thoughts. They were never real anyway. Next, I built positive programs in my head to "turn on the kickboxer." I constructed statements such as the following:

"Kickboxers lift weights for two hours a day."
"Kickboxers train for two hours a day at their dojo."
"Kickboxers ignore the pain of the moment for the inevitable glory that will be forever." Then all I had to do was be congruent with the presupposition. Because I was a kickboxer, I did those things. Sure, it took effort, but the logical process itself really was that simple. Next we will look at the emotional process.

Shifting Emotional State

You recall that your mammalian brain gives you access to instruction sets based on the emotional state you are in. Emotions result in memories and likewise, memories result in emotions; they are a package deal. The mammalian brain's assumption is that your emotional state will tell it what instructions will be most helpful at that time. This is how it gauges the context of what you are faced with in life. Let's say for example, you suddenly are faced with a very large dog. Context becomes a question of life or death. If you get scared, your mammalian brain will give you the "run like hell" instruction set. If the dog is your pet however, you will get happy when you see it, and your mammalian brain will give you the "stick hand out to pet dog" instruction set. For the mammalian brain, emotional context is everything.

Take the classic "guy cold approaching amazing girl at a nightclub" example. What is the number one thing an average guy will say when he sees an amazing girl he's attracted to? He will say that he wants to approach her, but that he has no clue what to say. Are you fucking kidding me? Can he speak English? What about "hello?" Would that be something he could say? Well dear reader, at least you understand what's really going on here. He doesn't expect the interaction to go well, so his mammalian brain is hiding the instruction set for how to start a conversation. It's really quite amusing, isn't it? He has actually forgotten how to say hello. OK, so let's get past this by using what we learned…

The guy sees an amazing girl he's attracted to. He cannot think of what to say. He knows that this is nothing more than his mammalian brain playing games with him. He starts walking toward the girl as he tells his mammalian brain, "Well, isn't this going to be awkward?" As he gets within conversation distance, he is nervous and everything about his body language says how nervous he is. Amazingly, he remembers how to say hello. She smiles (because of how nervous he looks) and says, "Ah, hi," and turns her back to him. He leaves.

At this point he will create a series of self-fulfilling prophecies based on how he chooses to perceive what happened. It's simply a game of Connect the Dots and it's all a domino effect of belief and emotion. It tends to be all or nothing, and without a reset, it will determine his reality for the rest of his life.

Reality #1 He was right. He walked up to the girl and said "hello." Just as he thought, she may have said "hi" back, but she wasn't interested in talking to him. He felt like a dork when she turned her back to him. He felt shame as he walked away. He doesn't ever want to feel like that again, so he is never going to do that again.

Reality #2 He was right. He knew that if he walked up to her, he would think of something to say. He successfully walked up to a girl no one else had the balls to walk up to and got her to say "hi" to him. It feels good to get past your fears and do what others are too scared to do. He has conquered the first challenge and knows what to expect next time. Now he is on to the second challenge: keeping her interested in talking. The next time he goes out and sees an amazing girl, he doesn't give his mammalian brain time to screw him up. He finds himself walking toward her right away. Because of this and the fact that he just did the same thing a few nights ago, he is more confident. He looks only about 60% as nervous as he looked last time. He is going to use a presupposition in his opener (because he knows that it could only help things). He walks up and says, "Hello, I'm Bob. I like talking to friendly girls and you looked friendly, so I had to come meet you." It works. She smiles. They talk for three minutes before she excuses herself to use the bathroom. Did he have sex with her? Nope. But look at what he did accomplish. He now "feels" as if he can start conversations with attractive women. The more he practices, the more he will learn and the further he will get. He doesn't see any failures; he just sees learning experience after learning experience as he gets better and better.

In either case, he chose his reality. His beliefs will only be reinforced as time goes on based on how he chooses to see things. He created an emotional loop and a self-fulfilling prophecy in either case. Emotion dictates the instructions that affect the outcome. The outcome tends to be interpreted based on the beliefs that created the original emotion. The original emotion gets stronger and so the cycle repeats. Now it's time to teach you how to logically pick the best base emotion so you can get the ball rolling in the right direction. A positive self-fulfilling prophecy is a good thing.

Consider this for a moment. Would a nervous-looking guy be getting great success with women? He is nervous because whatever he is doing is not working. As soon as the woman sees he is nervous, she knows that whatever he is about to do never works for him. The nervous guy has the woman believing he will fail before he even opens his mouth because she can see that he thinks he will fail.

So how do I approach an attractive woman? I start off with happy emotions. If I'm not already feeling them, all I have to do is remember the last time I approached an attractive woman and got good results. I remember the feelings. I remember how good it felt making her feel good. This memory gives me access to the most useful instruction sets hidden in my brain. It also gives me the correct body language. My body language will be congruent with my emotions. As I walk up, the woman sees my body language which tells her that what I am about to do works, and that I am successful with women. She can read whatever emotions I hold, and this reading affects how she responds. Then, when I am talking to her, I instantly humanize her, no matter how hot she is. Rather than getting the "oh my god, you are so hot that I don't know what to do" look on my face, I find some flaws right from the get-go. Admiring beauty is great, but I spend the first few seconds of the interaction figuring out things such as which ear is higher, how crooked her nose is, and how unsymmetrical her hairline is. As soon as I find a few imperfections, I cannot treat her as if she is perfect. She becomes a normal person who has the opportunity to have some fun with me. Think of this as my "I am successful with women, and you are just a normal woman" program.

So how can you start using this concept as in my personal example above? Always remember the first rule of reprogramming. Use only positive commands. Telling yourself to stop feeling nervous will only have the opposite effect. You need to tell yourself how to feel. You need to turn on the confidence and happy emotions. Ask yourself if you can remember a time when you were confident around women. Start small if you need to. Every guy will be able to find at least one memory if he reflects on it for a moment. All you need is just one anchor memory to build from. Think about that, and feel it as you enter the situation. This will up your odds for experiencing better results. Remember that there are no failures, only more information to help you get better and closer to your goal. As good interactions happen, add those to your stack of positive anchor memories to create a positive emotional feedback loop. You must focus. You can do this. For those of you wondering if the exact same thing applies in business, the answer is yes. It is all the same thing.

Steve and Phil just started working at Acme Advertising. They are both fresh out of college. After a little more than three weeks, the president of the company sends Steve an email. He wants to have lunch with Steve on Tuesday. When Steve sees this, he begins to wonder why. The only reason he can come up with is that he must be doing such a good job that the president wants to congratulate and reward him. Maybe he is going to get a quick promotion. Steve hasn't done anything much above the call of duty, but this is the only explanation he can come up with.

Phil gets the same email requesting lunch but on Wednesday. When Phil sees this, he begins to wonder why. The only reason he can come up with is that he must be doing something wrong, and the president wants to spend some time with him to get to the bottom of things. Maybe he is going to get fired. Phil hasn't screwed anything up, but this is the only explanation he can come up with.

The reality of the situation is that the president just enjoys any excuse to take a long lunch and have the company pay for it. He just likes "doing lunch," and it also gives him a chance to get to know his team. He really has no other motive than to stay out of the office and enjoy a free lunch.

Tuesday comes and Steve has lunch with the president. Lunch goes great. Steve is relaxed and joking with the president. By the end of the meal, you guessed it, no promotion, but they had some fun getting to know each other.

Wednesday comes and Phil has lunch with the president. Lunch doesn't go so well. Phil is fidgety and uncomfortable as he half-expects to get fired during the meal. By the end of the meal, you guessed it, he still has his job, but the president thinks Phil is a total weirdo.

On the following Thursday, the president meets with his CFO, who tells him that they need to make some immediate cutbacks. The CFO tells him that among other things, he is going to have to fire one of the two newest employees, Steve or Phil. Up until a few days ago, the decision would have been a coin toss. The president remembers the fun he had with Steve and the uncomfortable time he had with Phil. Who gets fired? Phil, the weirdo.

Life is 1% what happens to you and 99% how you respond to it. This is the equation from which you build your reality. Attitude is everything. What emotions are you building your reality with?

Emotions Are Contagious

The law of congruency says that the true self will always show through and that self is what will affect the people around you. If you want someone to feel something, you need to already be feeling it yourself. If you want everyone around you to be smiling, you need to feel it yourself. Over time, your reality becomes a mirror reflection of what is inside you. There is no escaping this, for better or for worse. This is why it is a bad idea to get angry with people, yell at people, or set yourself on paths of revenge, because all that dark energy has to originate in you before you can push it out onto other people. You cannot tarnish others without tarnishing yourself.

When I started my journey, I really hoped to find out that the tree-hugging "peace, love, and harmony" hippie stuff was a load of crap. What did I find out? It's not a load of crap. Really. It's all true. Sure, I can put my own personal edgy spin on it, as I have done in this book, but in the end, truth is truth. I tell you this because you need to know that one of the inescapable truths of the universe is simply that if you put negative things into the universe, you will get negative things back. If you put positive things into the universe, you will get positive things back. The monks figured this out thousands of years ago.

Ultimately your ability to persuade others will be limited only by your own congruency. Find positive emotional congruency and those around you will be persuaded into your reality.

The Empty Field

Your reality is mostly empty space filled in by what is in your head, like a game of Connect the Dots. People see your congruency by how you fill in that empty space. If you portray yourself as one thing and fill in that empty space with another, you are being incongruent, and that lowers the power with which you can communicate with those people. It's as if you are missing your own dots and where there should have been a picture of a car, you have drawn a banana. People will notice this kind of thing.

Let's look at this another way. Rather than a piece of paper with dots, consider a field with nothing but flat, empty space. Now consider how five different people would look at this same field. They are looking at the same empty space, but they will see completely different things.

The pilot whose plane just lost all engine power. _The pilot sees a perfect place to land safely. He has no future plans for this field past the next 10 minutes. All he wants to do is land safely and go home to his family._

The farmer. _The farmer sees a place to grow food. He is thinking long-term. He is wondering about things like soil density and composition._

The architect. *The architect sees a blank canvas on which to build a master-planned community. His vision will require years of effort by many, many people to bring to realization. One of the first things he will want to do with the land is to make some hills in a few select places. Perfectly flat is too boring. It's a good thing that he will not be doing this for a few years because hills would cause issues for the pilot.*

The land developer. *The land developer sees a place to build apartments and a shopping mall that he can lease out and make millions of dollars with. He will need to get some investors ASAP so that he can buy the land before some idiot turns it into farmland. What? There is a plane about to crash-land on it? Great, he can tell that story to the investors later. After he gets investors, he will need to find an architect. He hates dealing with architects, who are always inspired by the "art" they are creating while remaining clueless about budgets. All the developer cares about is how to get as many leasable square feet as possible at as high a lease rate as he can, all for the lowest build prices he can get.*

The environmentalist. *The environmentalist sees the current mating grounds of the brown-speckled shrike bird. He will sue the airline for crashing its plane here. He will also protest and*

352

try to stop the land developer. In the end, he will
prevent the architect from getting a job.
Eventually he will side with the farmer in an
attempt to save at least half of the mating grounds
of the brown-speckled shrike bird.

The point here is that they are all congruent in their unique ways. At no point did the pilot consider what was already in the field or what could be built on it while he was crash-landing his plane. The farmer just wants to grow food and has no clue how much money could be made building on the land. To the architect, it's just a blank canvas to put his work of art on. To the land developer, its just one of 72 different sections of land he is considering, and he has no clue what a brown-speckled shrike bird even looks like. Meanwhile, the environmentalist is going to go smoke some pot and forget about all of this until the next time he gets bored.

When you look out into your world, what do you see and how do you see it? Are all of your thoughts, actions, and emotions congruent?

Congruency Tests

Every single situation the world throws at you is a congruency test. Every conversation you have with someone is a congruency test. Every thought and every emotion that flows through you is a congruency test. You are what you are congruent with. You are as strong as the sum of your congruency. Without congruency, your value disappears. Your boss will test congruency. The attractive woman you are about to talk with will test congruency. The 16-year-old kid behind the counter at a 7-Eleven will test your congruency. Everyone tests your congruency, and they do it constantly.

It's the first day at the new job. Everything about Mark says that he is Mr. Go-getter Sales Guy! His new boss asks Mark to pick up his dry cleaning after he leaves work. Mark agrees, and Mark just lost the game. The new guy would not be picking up dry cleaning unless he thought he was low enough value that he had to do so. Mark wasn't congruent to being the big shot he was playing himself up to be.

The woman I have been talking to at the bar for the last five minutes asks me to buy her a drink. I tell her to make a small animal noise first. She heard what I said but is confused by my comment. I tell her that I will buy her a drink if she makes a small animal noise first. She laughs and makes a cat noise, not very well though. I put my hand on her shoulder and ask her to do it with feeling. She does it again, much better this time. I say, "OK, kitten, what do you want?" I just won the game. I set a precedent. If she wants something, she has to do something for me first, and if what she does fails to meet with my approval, she is not getting what she wants. I was congruent.

Larry is at the 7-Eleven bragging to the kid behind the counter about his new car while the kid grabs him some cigarettes. Larry explains that he just got paid on a big business deal and has crazy money in the bank right now. He then shows the kid Ferrari keys. When the kid goes to charge his ATM card for the cigarettes, AUTHORIZATION DECLINED. Larry doesn't have any other way to pay. The kid laughs at him because Larry is an incongruent jackass.

Why do people pay such close attention to congruency? The people you work with want to know if you will be able to perform as effectively as you lead them to believe you will. If the answer is no, it could affect the company in a way that could affect their jobs.

The woman you are with will test you because if you cannot stand up to her shit, how could she possibly expect you to protect her when the shit really does hit the fan? As for the kid at the 7-Eleven, well let's just say that he feels a lot better about himself now. He actually has enough money available on his ATM card to buy a pack of cigarettes.

The Ideal Self

It is impossible for something to be what it is not. The process we are talking about is not being, it is becoming. Being is where you are now. Becoming is the direction you are going right now. You have no control over the past, and it exists only in our minds anyway. Where you are right now is a result of the past, but you have no control over that anymore. Becoming is where the power is. What are you doing right now that guides you toward your destination? How congruent are you?

You need to hold a map in your head of your ideal self. Will this map be perfect? No map is, but it can still get you toward your goals. Ask yourself all the important questions. Who are you, ideally? What type of friends do you want, ideally? What about your job? Ideally, how do you want to spend your time? Where would you live? Play connect the dots and fill in the picture as best you can. Use this map to guide you and to keep you congruent. If it's not a place on your map, don't go there. Only travel the paths on the way to your destination. For any situation, ask how your ideal self would deal with it, and then do it that way, to the extent your current resources will allow. You will see that your life will begin to materialize **exactly** according to the map you are congruent with.

No man ever built a submarine while following the blueprints for an airplane. What blueprints are you following? And yes, you must follow the blueprints with 100% congruency, or all you will have is a hunk of metal that neither swims nor flies. Your life will be nothing more that the world's largest paperweight. So let me ask you, what color is your airplane? How will it feel to fly it? What is something you can do right now to start building it? Visualize existence and then take action.

Rock Star Dracula

Let's say that your ideal self is a rock star who dresses like Dracula. This is your reality, and you need to be 100% congruent with it. You will go out right now and buy a cape. You will wear this cape every day, starting today. If you can't play guitar, you will sign up for lessons right now. Go open the phone book and find a teacher. You will spend the next few months learning how to play. You are committed to spending the rest of your life getting better at it. Don't wait for a sale at Kmart. Go buy mascara now. Start doing everything you can to play the part until you are the part. Before you know it, when people say "Rock Star Dracula," everyone will think of you.

Of course society may condemn you for this role, but it's a big world and there is a place for everyone in it. The irony is that the weirder you are, the easier it is to claim your unique space in this world. Boring people don't get on TV talk shows, and the next person weirder than Marilyn Manson is sure to get a recording contract. Here is the best part. All of the attractive women who are bored with life (which is all of them) will secretly hope to be swept away by Rock Star Dracula. In time, you will have a harem of groupies.

Ultimately, people will take you as seriously as you portray yourself to be. Of course those who are not affected by you may make fun of you, but that doesn't matter because they are not part of your reality. You are congruent. This may be a ridiculous and extreme example, but it's also completely correct.

Choose Your Adventure

I'm sure the last eight weeks have been quite the adventure for you as you've put this stuff into action. I'm also sure that your experiences have made you love me at times and use my name as a curse word at others. Your eyes have been opened, you're not dead, and you have gained a wealth of information on communicating with power. This is where this books ends and where you choose what to do with your new toys. I may not know what you'll choose, but I do know that you're ready for it. Abandon your limiting beliefs, take action toward what you have decided you will have, and build your reality.

What to Do Next

You have just read *Power Communication: Secrets of the Alpha Male Book 2*. Go to my website at **www.drawkkwast.com/book3** to get the next book in the series, *Magnetic Interactions: Secrets of the Alpha Male Book 3*. While you're at my website, you can check out my blog, sign up for my newsletter and, if you're really serious about getting your shit together, have a look at Total Experience Immersion, listed under my training programs.

Acknowledgments

Shelton Keith Hill – Conceptual Proofreading

Mike Murray – Conceptual Proofreading

Jesse Murray – Conceptual Proofreading

Talia Murray – Proofreading

Dave Peyton – Proofreading

ProofreadingPal.com – Proofreading

Chazz Layne – Layout & Graphic Design

Ches Owen – Photography

CreateSpace.com – Printing and Distribution

Steve Aaronoff – Legal Consultant

Karl Roe – For surviving his friendship and becoming a better person because of it.

Garrett Mann – For knowing when to smile and when to roll his eyes at what I say.

John Montano – For knowing too much was just enough.

John Korinko – For putting up with my bullshit and keeping me on track.

Brad Chapman – For being a grounding rod and my last fail-safe.

Tommy Demichele – The original "Rock Star Dracula."

David Atkins – Because nothing feels better than helping those who have helped you.